How the Blacks *Created* CANADA

At any time in the last half of the 20th century a book with this title would have been met with disbelief at best and at worst derision. The "conventional wisdom "for some time has been that there was no significant history of the black communities in Canada worth telling.

With this book that features a selection of intriguing profiles of outstanding black Canadians, the author has presented a powerful challenge to that old limited perspective. Building on efforts undertaken over the years by a small band of writers, librarians, academics, public historians and modern-day griots (African keepers of oral history) to keep these stories alive, Fil Fraser has offered us an intriguing and unusual gift.

It is one that provides readers with easy access to important aspects of our country's history about which most Canadians have been for the most part completely unaware.

It is a gift that has the potential to stimulate some fundamental shifts in our personal perceptions about our country and its ongoing difficult efforts to create a prosperous, inclusive, caring and truly multicultural society.

It is a gift full of exciting surprises about the role of members of the various black communities in the development of Canada in the more than 400 years that they have been part of our mosaic.

While acknowledging that the stories of these black communities has often been one of trials and tribulations, the authors special contribution is to present us with powerful stories—covering the period from 1600 to the present—of outstanding leadership by black Canadians. He invites us to celebrate these achievements and to draw on them for inspiration in our own lives.

This gift is a timely one; it will understandably be welcomed by members of the present-day African Canadian communities who are eager to know their own particular stories. It will also be welcomed by educators, by community leaders, by museum directors and by social activists and policy makers who are eager to strengthen a full awareness of our diverse histories and the behaviours and actions needed to create harmonious communities out of this diversity.

It will be welcomed as well by anyone who is hungry for inspirational stories of leadership that demonstrates evidence of courage, resilience, discipline, creativity and respect for others in building sustainable communities.

In that sense it is a gift for all Canadians and a gift for all ages. We are indebted to Fil Fraser for this precious gift.

—Donald Simpson Ph,D, Chief Explorer, Innovation Expedition Inc.; Innovator in Residence, The Harriet Tubman Institute for Research on the Global Migration of African Peoples; Author, *Under the North Star : Black Communities in Upper Canada Before 1867*

How the
Blacks
Created
CANADA

FIL FRASER

DRAGON
HILL

The Publisher: Dragon Hill Publishing Ltd.

Library and Archives Canada Cataloguing in Publication

Fraser, Fil, 1932–
    How the Blacks created Canada / Fil Fraser.
Includes bibliographical references.

ISBN 978-1-896124-43-8
1. Blacks—Canada—History. 2. Black Canadians—History. I. Title.

FC106.B6F73   2009971'.00496   C2009-906022-1

Project Director: Gary Whyte
Project Editor: Kathy van Denderen
Cover Image: Commemorative stamp images courtesy of Canada Post Corporation:
Portia White: Irrepressible Talent, 46¢. © Canada Post Corporation; issued 17 December 1999. Reproduced with Permission.
Oscar Peterson, 50¢, © Canada Post Corporation; issued 15 August 2005. Reproduced with Permission.
Josiah Henson, 1789–1883, 32¢. © Canada Post Corporation; issued 16 September 1983. Reproduced with Permission.
Rosemary Brown, 54¢. © Canada Post Corporation; issued 2 February 2009. Reproduced with Permission.
William Hall, V.C., 57¢. © Canada Post Corporation; issued 1 February, 2010. Reproduced with Permission.
Photo Credits: Every effort has been made to accurately credit the sources of photographs. Any errors or omissions should be reported directly to the publisher for correction in future editions. Photographs courtesy of Anthony Fields (p. 166); Donald Oliver (p. 105); Hank Boer (p.p. 33,35); Fil Fraser (pp. 79, 157, 188, 193, 199, 229); George Elliott Clarke (p. 107); Glenbow Museum (pp. 77, 81, 88); Gordon Sedawie, *Vancouver Province* (p. 211); *Hymn to Freedom* (pp. 63, 72, 83, 84, 97, 101, 112, 113, 115, 122, 125); Library and Archives Canada (p. 26, PA-61930); Photos.com (chapter intros); University of Alberta (p. 175).

We acknowledge the support of the Alberta Foundation for the Arts for our publishing program.

CONTENTS

Dedication

*If someone says that you're not as good as they are, prove to
them that they are wrong.*

—Felix Paul Blache-Fraser

To the courageous and determined women and men
who overcame every kind of obstacle to make meaningful
contributions to the creation of Canada, and upon whose
shoulders we proudly stand.

ACKNOWLEDGEMENTS

My real writing career started because of Grant Kennedy, the founder of Lone Pine Publishing. During lunch at the University of Alberta Faculty Club a few years back, we were talking about a short story I had written when I said, "You only know you're a writer when someone else says you are." "Well," he replied, "would you consider yourself a writer if someone offered you an advance to write a book?"

The book was *Alberta's Camelot: Culture and the Arts in the Lougheed Years*, published in 2003. So my first thanks go to Grant Kennedy, now happily retired on the Sunshine Coast but still a significant influence in Canadian publishing.

Camelot was followed three years later by *Running Uphill: The Fast, Short Life of Canadian Champion Harry Jerome*, which became the basis for a feature documentary film produced by the National Film Board of Canada. It was Denham Jolly, the first Black owner of a radio station in Canada, who encouraged me to write the biography of Harry Jerome. But it was Almeta Speaks who, a decade earlier, introduced me to a part of Canadian history of which I was largely unaware, by hiring me as the narrator/host of *Hymn to Freedom,* a four-hour documentary history of Blacks in Canada. I owe both of them a debt of gratitude.

Gary Whyte, publisher of Dragon Hill Publishing Ltd., rose to the occasion and managed the publication of *Running Uphill* within a short time frame, allowing me to present the first copy to Governor General Michaëlle Jean at the Harry Jerome Awards in Toronto in April 2006. And now, *How the Blacks Created Canada,* also published by Dragon Hill, has deepened my perception of the role of minorities in Canada and reinforced my love for this still imperfect but remarkably wonderful country.

Many members of the Black community, friends, associates and former strangers, opened their hearts, their papers and their libraries to me as I gathered the stories that make up this book. I especially want to thank Mairuth Sarsfield, a distinguished author in her own right, who shared insights and information with me. There are many others, too many to mention here, who should know how much I appreciated their interest and encouragement.

Through it all, my publisher, Gary Whyte, and his associates have given me extraordinary support with their appreciation and respect for my work and their efforts to make readers aware of my books. My thanks to Kathy van Denderen, my editor, whose work on the manuscript for this book has been both efficient and professional.

Finally, I'm not kidding when I say that none of this would have been possible without the limitless and unwavering support of my loving wife of 27 years, Gladys Carol Odegard.

FOREWORD

A complete account of the Black contribution to Canada is long overdue. There are academic treatises, articles and biographies of Black Canadians who made their mark on our country. There are artifacts, photographs and journals in museums and archives that depict the Black experience. But until now, there has never been a book that traces the many achievements of Black individuals and communities from sea to shining sea. At last, the wait is over.

For more than 400 years, Blacks have been an integral part of the warp and weave of this great country. For example, as an interpreter between the French and the Mi'kmaq people in the early 1600s, Mathieu Da Costa played a vital role in developing the fur-trade industry in Canada. Da Costa was a freeman. Those who came after him, enslaved and brutally exploited during the largest shift of population that the world has ever seen, however, played no less an important, if often ignored or forgotten, role in shaping Canada.

Thanks to Fil Fraser's *How the Blacks Created Canada*, our role can no longer be ignored or forgotten. This book is a "celebration of achievement" from the story of how a small Black community saved British Columbia for Canada, to the trials and triumphs of Blacks in Upper Canada, to the profound influence of the Black church in Nova Scotia. Blacks, through the sheer force of character and a never satisfied appetite for change, transformed this nation. They paved the way forward for the "icons and trailblazers" of today who continue to define Canada.

You will read in this book about the many Black Canadians who made contributions that count—to the arts and Canadian culture, to Canadian laws and policies and to Canada's status on the world stage. When you consider the magnificent splendour of their collective accomplishments, however, I hope you will come to appreciate the most important contribution of Black Canadians.

I believe that Black Canadians, through their struggle for equality, dignity and a clear, strong voice, have played a central role in helping to create a Canada that is more diverse, more inclusive and more welcoming to other cultures. To be sure, the struggle continues. But just as surely, Blacks have made, and continue to make, critical advancements. For that, all Canadians should be grateful, and all Black Canadians should be proud.

That's because the full impact of the work of Black Canadians in helping to create a more diverse and inclusive Canada is more important now than ever before. Diverse and inclusive countries attract the best talent. By bringing together different cultures and experiences, these countries become hubs of innovation and creativity. Their industries prosper. Their cultures thrive. And their societies become more compassionate.

The great Dr. Martin Luther King once observed: "Almost always, the creative dedicated minority has made the world better." This book vividly underscores how one such creative dedicated minority, Black Canadians, did indeed make our world a better place. Our journey, the journey of all Canadians, continues.

As such, I hope that *How the Blacks Created Canada* will encourage all Canadians to build bridges among the more than 200 different ethnic groups in our country today. I hope it will help Canadians to recognize the importance of understanding and tolerance. And most of all, I hope it will inspire others to strive to make a difference.

–Hon. Donald H. Oliver, Q.C.

PREFACE

YES, HISTORY MADE YOU:
NOW, GO MAKE HISTORY!

For Howard Douglas McCurdy, PhD (1932–)

Africans—Black people—Negroes, by whatever name, from whatever roots or routes, created the possibility for modernity, for being "new" and "advanced" and achieving "progress." Our present world—globalized by commerce and mass media—began to emerge half a millennium ago, when African peoples were captured and forced onto European vessels and then surged into the Americas to mine gold and silver, harvest sugar cane and cotton, nurture their masters' families, and entertain all with song and jests.

Some are ashamed—or feel victimized—by this history. We need not be. Obviously, those first "New World" Africans were hardy, superb, intelligent, spirited and industrious. They survived the horrors of rape, infanticide, torture, gross abuse and casual massacres, as well as the crimes of lynch law, two-faced religion, scorched-earth destitution and unlettered tutoring. Not only did they survive, but they also gave the world new forms of speech, advanced styles of music and a superior theology.

But let the history books also show that our ancestors, those stolen and exploited Africans, through their sweat, constructed Western Europe: they financed the Renaissance, paid for the launching of globe-carving, imperialist navies and heaped up the capital necessary to inaugurate the Industrial Revolution. It was their determination, too, to seize their liberty that fostered transcendent arguments over freedom and tyranny, revolution and the rule of law, democracy and aristocracy/elitism, white supremacy and anti-racism. Their struggle insisted upon the innate dignity of humanity, a concept essential to any notion of liberation.

Their desire for liberty also gave birth to nations: Crispus Attucks was the first rebel to die in the American Revolution; but 3500 other African Americans fled the Republic for British North America, thus becoming "a founding people" of what became Canada. Then, the slaves of San Domingo rose up, throwing out their French masters and founding Haiti, the world's first Black republic. Soon, other "overseas" Africans were returning to the continent, helping to establish Sierra Leone and Liberia.

In the 20th century, the Harlem Renaissance and Marcus Garvey's Universal Negro Improvement Association espoused Pan-Africanist and Black Pride theories that nourished independence movements in Africa and the Caribbean and that then returned to North America as Civil Rights Movement activism and Black Power agitation. In turn, these intellectual and socio-political engagements supported the liberation of South Africa from *apartheid* rule, electing Nelson Mandela president there, and inspired the construction of a "dream coalition" that installed an African American, Barack Obama, in the White House.

But Fil Fraser's focus is Canada, this "astonishing country," as he says, and one which owes an astonishingly unacknowledged debt to its citizens of African/Negro ancestry. Not only because our ancestors were enslaved in five of the original colonies (Nova Scotia, New Brunswick, Prince Edward Island, Nouvelle-France/Quebec, and Upper Canada/Ontario), but also because our free ancestors helped to buttress colonial Canada against potential and actual American invasion.

Writing in 1852, the U.S.-born, African Canadian abolitionist Mary Ann Shadd proposed that free African Americans emigrate *en masse* to Canada West (Ontario) or British Columbia, not just to escape the reach of the pernicious U.S. Fugitive Slave Law, but to "garrison" (her exact word) these lands against the Republic's insatiable appetite for new slaveholding territory. She saw clearly that it was in Black self-interest to keep colonial British North America (Canada) safe from American expansionism and to "keep up the balance of power": African Americans needed to back British imperialism—tactically, to contain and defeat American slavery—strategically.

Even though vast thousands of African Americans who entered British North America before the U.S. Civil War never read, presumably, a single word that Shadd wrote, their presence and their anti-slavery inclinations did serve, as Fraser discusses, to help keep British North America "British," or, rather, to make it more possible for these colonies to confederate into Canada.

Scholars state that the American Revolution created both the United States and Canada—the latter as a kind of reactionary, anti-republican state. But Canada was also shaped by the anti-slavery strategies that brought visionary emancipationists like Harriet Tubman to its "Dominion," and this legacy is radical. Indeed, the Canadian tradition of "progressive conservatism"—that ultra-soft socialism—owes something to anti-slavery rhetoric.

But such history is always only a prelude. Fil Fraser's *How the Blacks Created Canada* demonstrates, with narrative zeal, stylistic panache and attractive wit how Blacks have consistently defined and redefined "The Great White North," from putting our stamp on geography (Amber Valley and Africville) to making our mark on the state (Lincoln Alexander and Michäelle Jean). Yes, the list of accomplishments and of the accomplished is long. But it will be even longer once we have recovered much of our hidden history and once you—*you*—have blazed upon our era your good name and your stellar deeds.

George Elliott Clarke, OC, ONS, PhD
E.J. Pratt Professor of Canadian Literature
University of Toronto

INTRODUCTION

Across geography and across time, Blacks have played pivotal roles in the creation of Canada. But while their achievements are gradually being chronicled in a developing library of both popular and scholarly works, with rare exceptions, that history has been virtually invisible to mainstream Canadians. Black immigrants and refugees from the United States, from the Caribbean and from Africa, like those from many other parts of the world, have endured a soul-sapping storm of prejudice and discrimination. But in the age of Obama, as Blacks (like the Irish, the Ukrainians, the Italians and others who struggled to join the Anglo-centric mainstream before them) begin to emerge as fully integrated citizens, it's time for all Canadians to know who they are. It's time to celebrate the contributions and achievements of those whose roots in our soil are as deep as anyone else's.

Without a substantial Black community there is persuasive evidence that, before joining Confederation, British Columbia might have been lost to the United States. The record shows that in 1858, James Douglas invited some 800 former American slaves and freemen to settle in Victoria. At a critical moment in history, they became the majority non-Native population of what was then a British outpost, staving off the potential threat of an America that might have stretched from California to Alaska.

Six thousand kilometres to the east, at the dawn of Canadian history, African navigator Mathieu Da Costa, acting as a guide and interpreter, eased the way for Samuel de Champlain's explorations. His pioneering knowledge of Aboriginal languages facilitated communication between Europeans and the First Nations of North America. Da Costa is reported to have been fluent in Dutch, English, French and Portuguese as well as Aboriginal languages. He was the first free Black to come to what would become Canada.

In the 1770s, Blacks who moved to Nova Scotia with the United Empire Loyalists became Canada's largest Black community. Portia White, one of our country's most internationally acclaimed singers, and the contemporary opera star, Measha Brueggergosman, are both descendants of the Black Loyalists community.

In Ontario, Josiah Henson's historical homestead near what is now Dresden, Ontario, is a reminder of Dawn, a vibrant community that he led after coming to Canada through the storied Underground Railway, leaving behind half a lifetime of slavery. Harriet Beecher Stowe's bestselling novel, *Uncle Tom's Cabin,* was inspired by Henson's life story.

A later descendant of the migrants who had followed the "north star" to freedom, the gifted composer Nathaniel Dett, born in Drummondville (now Niagara Falls), Ontario, in 1882, left a legacy of works that are part of Canada's classical music repertoire. The respected Nathaniel Dett Chorale performs today on radio and television and in concerts across the country.

In the early years of the 20th century, Black settlements dotted the prairies. Settlements near Maidstone, Saskatchewan, like others at Breton and Wildwood in Alberta, saw the development of thriving communities by Blacks who had come north from the U.S.

The past and present role of Blacks in sports and entertainment is well known. Harry Jerome and Donovan Bailey, Oscar Peterson and Oliver Jones are all national icons. In 1955, when television was literally still black and white, Eleanor Collins, whose family came from Oklahoma at the turn of the 20th century, became the first woman of any colour to host her own national television program, *The Eleanor Show,* on the CBC.

In Ontario, Lincoln Alexander became the first Black lieutenant-governor in Canada, while Jean Augustine, the first Black woman to be elected to the House of Commons, served as a cabinet minister and as deputy prime minister under Jean Chrétien.

Many others names are woven into the fabric of Canadian history: John Ware, Alberta's famous Black cowboy; Mary Ann Shadd, the first Black newspaper publisher in North America; and author Carrie Best, whose biography, *The Lonesome Road,* won international acclaim. The record of achievement includes human rights activist Rosemary Brown, Chief Justice Julius Isaac, broadcaster/businessman Denham Jolly, MP Howard McCurdy, Senator Donald Oliver, hockey's

Herb Carnegie, Giller Prize–winning author Austin Clarke, Governor General's Award for Poetry winner George Elliott Clarke, Ontario Human Rights Commission leader Daniel G. Hill and his famous sons, musician Dan Jr. ("Sometimes When We Touch") and author Lawrence, whose *The Book of Negroes* won the 2009 Commonwealth Book Prize, to name a few.

One cannot, of course, overlook the Governor General of Canada; the Right Honourable Michaëlle Jean, a Haitian refugee, has brought incandescent luminosity to the highest office in the land.

Anthropologically speaking, we are all children of Africa. Lucy, the name attributed to the oldest human skeleton discovered, lived some three million years ago and is, figuratively, grandmother to us all. Anthropologists tell us that Africa was the crèche of the human race. It's at best ironic, at worst tragic, that the role of Africa's modern descendents in the development of the Western world has been largely unheralded. Much of what has been written and reported on Blacks has focused on stories of prejudice and racism that cry out to be told; from pre-Confederation Canadian slavery to the current, almost apocryphal offence of DWB: Driving While Black. Word on the Toronto street is that if you're Black and drive a good car, be very careful around certain police officers and in certain neighbourhoods.

But this book is not about racism and discrimination. It is a celebration of achievement, which is a much better story. There are literally thousands of Black Canadians, women and men in all parts of the country who are modern pioneers, breaking down walls of prejudice, opening new doors and creating vocational and professional pathways that others will surely follow. The tough reality for the writer is that they cannot all be included in this book. To properly chronicle the lives and contributions of all of the Black men and women who have contributed to the creation of Canada would expand this volume to encyclopaedic proportions. (Did you know that when Prince George, BC, celebrates Black History Month, a steel pan band is at the centre of the event?) Inevitably, people who should be included will be left out. For this, I apologize.

Black icons include community builders, politicians and physicians, athletes and musicians, authors and actors, scientists and inventors, academics and business leaders. All have helped to create Canada by changing perceptions through education and example, making the country more inclusive and better able to manage the diversity that defines the way we see ourselves.

Finally, a word about terminology. I have chosen to use the term "Black," capitalized, to refer to a people who have, across time, been variously described as Negroes, Coloureds and Afro or African Canadians, not to mention a stinging variety of less salutary terms. There has been some controversy about whether the term "African Canadian" (a northern echo of the workable "African American") covers the whole demographic. Clear distinctions can be drawn between the Blacks who came early with the British Empire Loyalists, those who escaped slavery through the Underground Railway, and those who, generations later, emigrated from the West Indies and modern Africa. It is my view that "Black," at least in this era, best describes to the largest audience who we are. The term has been rescued from the derogatory stink of earlier times and given a proud spin by the present generation.

You may also notice that I use the term "mainstream Canadians" to describe the demographic majority of our population. I refer specifically to white, Anglo-Saxon and Anglo-Celtic Canadians and those Europeans who fit comfortably into a culture with middle-class democratic values. Many with eastern or southern European roots now perceive themselves as part of the mainstream. But "mainstream" still does not, at this stage of our country's development, include visible minorities or First Nations people.

This is not to say that minority persons cannot feel themselves to be part of the mainstream and subscribe to its core values. But we are not a melting pot. As a lifelong broadcaster and journalist, I have always worked and lived successfully in the mainstream. In fact, it is thanks to Denham Jolly, the creator of the Harry Jerome Awards, that, in my 70s, quite late in life, I really became seriously involved for the first time in the issues Black Canadians faced. I am profoundly grateful to both Jolly and to my publisher, who encouraged me to research and write the present volume, for steering me into a profound appreciation of Canadian life and realities.

How the Blacks Created Canada, published by Dragon Hill Publishing, places the contributions of ethnic groups in building Canada in a modern perspective. This and other books published by Dragon Hill are fitting recognition of the diversity of people who are the bedrock of this remarkable country. It is my hope that these books will surprise and delight Canada's maturing mainstream audiences.

CHAPTER ONE

SAVING
BRITISH COLUMBIA
FOR CANADA

I t is at once the most dramatic and the least well-known story in Canadian history. Imagine Canada without a west coast, with the United States stretching up the Pacific from California to Alaska. What kind of country would we be if our western boundary began on the eastern slopes of the Rocky Mountains, stretching from sea to shining mountains? Few know how close we came to that possibility.

Consider pre-Confederation Canada in the mid-1840s. Aside from settlements in what decades later would become Lower and Upper Canada, Rupert's Land, the vast territory to the north and west, was mostly the fur-trading preserve of the competing North West and Hudson's Bay companies. Under licence from the British crown, the two companies traded for furs from forts located across the far north all the way to the Pacific and extending south to include the basin of the Columbia River. Fort Vancouver, the Hudson's Bay Company's principal western fur-trading post, was set on the banks of the Columbia River, across from present-day Portland, Oregon. The largest river in the Pacific northwest rises in Canada from Columbia Lake in the Kootenay Valley. The Columbia River flows north through Golden, then turns south, passing through Revelstoke on its 2000-kilometre journey to the Pacific. Within its 670,000-square-kilometre basin, the river envelops both Oregon and what is now the state of Washington.

The Oregon Territory had for many years been a matter of dispute between Britain and the U.S., with both claiming the territory. James Douglas, appointed governor for what was then the Crown Colony of Vancouver Island, was becoming concerned about the increasing American population south of the Columbia River. A provisional U.S. government had been established at Wilmette, across the river from Fort Vancouver. "An American population will never willingly submit to British domination," Douglas wrote, "and it would be ruinous and hopeless to enforce obedience, on a disaffected people; our Government would not attempt it, and the consequence will be the accession of a new State to the Union." With so many settlers pouring into the West, "Every sea port will be converted into a naval arsenal and the Pacific covered with swarms of Privateers, to the destruction of British commerce in those seas."

By 1845, the white population in Oregon had grown to some 6000. There were rumblings of war as many Americans believed that their country's manifest destiny was to stretch from Panama to the Arctic. American president, James K. Polk, had won the 1844 election on a chest-thumping platform of "Fifty-four Forty or Fight." While the United States saw the West as a territory to settle, Great Britain viewed the vast northern hinterland mainly as a treasure trove of beaver pelts. With the border at 54°40' North, western Canada would have been an arctic preserve with the U.S. encompassing Vancouver Island, Edmonton, Winnipeg and lower Hudson Bay.

An awakened Britain responded to the U.S. with a proposal that the border follow the 49th parallel across the prairies to a point near what is now Trail, BC, and then follow the Columbia River to the Pacific, setting the river as the southern border of what was to become Canada. The Americans would have none of it. They began to form militia units and threatened to storm Hudson's Bay forts. The Royal Navy established a force at Esquimalt.

In the end, the British foreign secretary, Lord Aberdeen, negotiated an agreement to set the border along the 49th parallel, essentially from Lake Superior to the Pacific, with an arrangement that would see all of Vancouver Island remain under British rule. A strange anomaly left Point Roberts, which has no land connection to the U.S., as part of the United States. The Treaty of Washington was signed on June 15, 1846, seemingly resolving the issue and leading to the creation of the state of Washington.

But in the 1840s, Canada was still decades away from becoming a country, and in the Wild West, anything was possible. Pressure mounted as, after gold was discovered in California in 1848, a torrent of Americans flooded west. During the next year, hordes of fortune seekers (heralded as the quasi-mythical "49ers"), fuelled by stories of people picking up gold nuggets the size of goose eggs off the ground, came in search of a quick fortune. Some reports say that as many as 80,000 adventurers poured into California.

After a romantically storied decade, as the gold that had lured the 49ers to California petered out, rumours surfaced of another find near Yale in the Fraser River Canyon. The news spread like wildfire after it leaked out that, early in 1858, James Douglas had sent a shipment of the yellow metal to San Francisco to be refined. The 49ers swarmed northward to cash in on the discovery and, as a consequence, opened a frontier for what some believed should have been part of the American West. Britain needed to take dramatic action to maintain control of the territory, and Douglas, one of the most formidable leaders in Canadian history, was the man to do it. As Crawford Killian put it in *Go Do Some Great Thing: The Black Pioneers of British Columbia,* "Had anyone else attempted to govern the new colony during the 1850s and early 1860s, it is likely that British Columbia—perhaps all of western Canada—would have become part of the United States."

Britain established the Crown Colony of Vancouver Island in 1849, leasing the entire island to the Hudson's Bay Company. In August 1858, on Douglas' urgent recommendation, the Crown Colony of British Columbia was created to include and formalize Britain's claims to the mainland. James Douglas, acknowledged as the Father of British Columbia, was installed as the governor of both colonies.

OLD SQUARE TOES

James Douglas had worked his way across the west and up though the ranks to become the chief factor of the Hudson's Bay Company's main trading centre at Fort Vancouver. With pressure from the Americans mounting, he recommended that Britain establish a new western base on the southern tip of Vancouver Island. He had selected Victoria as the site in 1842 and supervised construction of the new fort the following year. In 1849, after nearly 20 years at Fort Vancouver, Douglas moved his family north and set about building the capital for the Crown Colony of Vancouver Island at Fort Victoria.

With the onset of the major thrust of the Fraser Canyon gold rush in the spring of 1858, Douglas and his British masters worried that the American influx would put their claim to what is now British Columbia in jeopardy. In the 19th century, territorial claims were confirmed through settlement. And with as many as 30,000 would-be miners and the touts who lived off their avails heading north for the jumping-off spot at Fort Victoria, he needed settlers right away.

It has never been clearly established how much a factor Douglas' own racial background influenced the ensuing events. Douglas' personal heritage is fascinating in its own right. He was born on August 15, 1803, the second of three children born in British Guiana to a Black mother and a Glaswegian father. James' mother, Martha Ann Tefler, originally from Barbados, was *free coloured*, which in her time and place meant a free person of mixed European and African ancestry. The reality she and other "mulattos" or "Creoles" faced was that if any part of you is Black, and it shows, Black is how the world sees you. James and his siblings, an older brother Alexander and his sister Cecilia, were taken to Great Britain by their father, John Douglas, and given British educations. Martha Ann, who had business interests of her own, remained in Guiana. It was typical of colonial liaisons of the era that James' parents lived together and had children but never married.

Alexander turned out to be physically frail and of limited intelligence. But James was tall and ruggedly muscular even as a young teenager. At preparatory school in Scotland, he developed a reputation as a hard-hitting scrapper who never backed down from a fight. When he was 16, James joined the North West Company as an apprentice, displaying both a capacity for focused hard work and an inquisitive, analytical intelligence. He rose quickly through the ranks at fur-trading stations across the west, from Fort William at the head of Lake Superior to Isle a la Cross to Fort Vermillion to Fort St. James, and he eventually became chief factor at Fort Vancouver. He learned accounting, became expert in the business

Sir James Douglas, the Father of British Columbia, sometimes known as "Old Square Toes," was a tough administrator who prevented BC from falling into American hands.

methods of the fur trade and carefully studied the character of the various Native tribes, the company's indispensable suppliers. James studied history and politics and nearly made a fetish of observing the minutest details of every transaction, at the same time displaying an unrelenting commitment to punctuality. He was, in short, the perfect company man.

Douglas' complexion reflected his ancestry, and it's likely that most of his contemporaries were aware of his mixed racial heritage. Some fur traders reportedly referred to him as a "Scotch West Indian." His heritage does not, however, seem to be a fact he either emphasized or dwelt upon. His own marriage to Amelia Connolly, daughter of an Irish-Cree union, indicated that racial differences were unimportant to him. And the fur-trading companies showed little concern for racial background—what counted was ability, loyalty and hard work. Like many European members of the fur-trading companies, Douglas had "married" Amelia according to Native customs—*à la façon du pays*, meaning "in the fashion of the country." It was only after the birth of several children that the marriage, which seems to have been a lifelong love affair, was solemnized in a Christian ceremony.

The Father of British Columbia was a no-nonsense autocrat who ruled with absolute authority and an imperious air that was almost cartoonish. Some dubbed him "Old Square Toes."

In the spring of 1858, the need for settlers in Fort Victoria was urgent. And the most readily available candidates were Blacks—former slaves and freemen who had migrated from the perilous American south to California, which had declared itself a free state. Alas, for the "coloured" migrants, the state was far from free.

Laws were passed that, among other things, prohibited a Black man from testifying in court against a white man. Black voting rights, which seemed to exist on paper—all residents had to pay a poll tax—were never real. Legislation allowing newly arrived slave owners to retain their "property" was being advanced in spite of the state's constitutional prohibitions against slavery. In March, the legislature took up a bill to restrict the immigration of Negroes, requiring them to register. Racism was alive and thriving in the "free state." Having escaped from slavery, having endured and often prospered, the Blacks, who owned taxable property estimated at $5 million in value, found their status as citizens to be, at best, flimsy.

On the evening of April 14, 1858, Jeremiah Nagle, captain of the *Commodore,* a side-wheeler steamship that sailed between San Francisco and Victoria, attended a mass meeting held at the Black Zion Church in San Francisco. The congregation, in the face of mounting racism, was urgently considering mass emigration to Panama, to the Mexican state of Sonora, or to the Colony of Vancouver Island. Nagle, with Douglas' approval, invited the group to come north. He brandished maps and a letter from "a gentleman in the service of the Hudson's Bay Company of undoubted veracity." The immigrants would be given British subject status, the right to vote and own property and would eventually be eligible for British citizenship.

Less than a week later, on April 20, an advance party of some 35 members of the congregation embarked for Victoria aboard the *Commodore.* Their mission was to meet with Governor James Douglas to confirm that life under the British flag would be better. A hopeful wharfside gathering of almost the entire Black population of

San Francisco saw them off. After a rough five-day voyage, the *Commodore* docked at Victoria on a warm spring day. The peach trees were in bloom, and the profligate vegetation that can take your breath away when you fly in today from points east was almost wantonly lush.

Upon disembarking at Victoria, some members of the delegation knelt in prayer, seeking heavenly blessing for a new life of freedom under the protective paw of the British lion. Their hope for a better future was only slightly dimmed by the presence of their fellow passengers aboard Captain Nagle's ship, about 450 white men heading for the gold fields.

The delegates sent word back to San Francisco that they had found "one of the garden spots of the world." Vancouver Island was "a place which has unfolded to us in our darkest hour." Douglas gave them a warm welcome and confirmed that they could buy land for a pound per acre with 25 percent down and the balance to be paid within four years. After nine months as property owners, they had the right to vote and to serve on juries. And when they completed seven years as residents, they could apply for British citizenship. Reverend Edward Cridge, the Anglican chaplain to the Hudson's Bay Company also warmly entertained the delegation. Cridge invited them to join his congregation, promising that they would be accepted without discrimination.

Upon getting the news, Blacks in San Francisco created an emigration company, and some 400 families followed the original delegation to a new life in British Columbia. By the end of 1858, some 800 Blacks had made the move to Victoria. (Various accounts have put the number somewhere between 600 and 1000.) Many sold their California properties, often at a loss, but they arrived at their new home with sufficient resources to buy land

and set up businesses. Within two years, members of the Black community, both literate and skilled, were reported to own property valued, for taxation purposes, at an estimated 50,000 pounds.

Among the immigrants were Samuel Ringo, who operated restaurants and other businesses; Joshua Howard, who offered legal services; Willis Bond, a former slave who became a property owner, a contractor and an auctioneer; and several people with accreditation as teachers. Bond was later described by the Speaker of the Vancouver Island Assembly as "one of the cleverest men white or black that I have ever met." The former slaves had found a new home where they were accepted and could live as full citizens.

There are conflicting reports as to whether one of the members of the first advance party was Mifflin Wistar Gibbs. But it's certain that he was one of the earliest immigrants to the colony who soon became one of the most respected leaders of the Black community. A well-educated businessman, he and his partner, Peter Lester, had operated The Pioneer Boot and Shoe Emporium in San Francisco, which, in spite of some ugly racial incidents, had been very successful. Both men had fought slavery and were dedicated to improving the lot of Blacks in America.

Gibbs was born in Philadelphia in 1828, the son of a Methodist minister. As a young man, he helped escaped slaves and freemen navigate the Underground Railway through Pennsylvania to southern Ontario. By the time he was 20, he had joined the Black abolitionists, Charles Lennox Remond and the legendary Frederick Douglass, on an anti-slavery speaking circuit. Gibbs petitioned the Pennsylvania government for Blacks to have the right to vote. The lure of California, which had declared itself a free state, took him to San Francisco in 1850. Literally starting from scratch, he began earning his living shining shoes. It wasn't long before his entrepreneurial talent saw him opening a store that successfully sold imported boots and shoes from London and New York. In California he honed his political activism and, in 1855, became the founder of San Francisco's first Black newspaper, the *Mirror of the Times,* edited by a leading Black intellectual, William H. Newby. The newspaper was dedicated to advocating equal rights and denounced a series of recently enacted "black laws" that made a mockery of California's free state status. In 1857, Gibbs and Lester refused to pay a state poll tax unless they were allowed to vote, sparking a battle that saw them attacked and beaten in their own store. They barely avoided the confiscation of their property.

Given his demonstrated entrepreneurial skills, it should come as no surprise that Gibbs arrived in Victoria with an inventory of boots, picks and shovels and other mining supplies that promptly sold out. He immediately sent word to Lester in San Francisco to send more. Gibbs bought a house for $3000 that became the site for a mercantile business, reportedly the first outside the Hudson's Bay Company. The firm of "Lester and Gibbs—Dealers in Groceries, Provisions, Boots, Shoes, etc., Wholesale & Retail" became a serious competitor to the Bay's own store. Gibbs bought more property and prospered as both a businessman and a community leader. In addition to other ventures, he became a director of the Queen Charlotte Coal Company. He eventually resigned the directorship so that he could bid on a contract from the company, which he won. In January 1859, with 50 men, he headed north to the Queen Charlotte Islands to build a railway and wharves from the coalmine to Skidgate Harbour.

He shipped "the first cargo of anthracite coal ever unearthed on the Pacific seaboard."

Gibbs was not totally preoccupied with business; his involvement in community and political affairs is the most important part of his legacy. When James Douglas created a House of Assembly for the Crown Colony of Vancouver Island in 1860, in keeping with the times, the right to vote was restricted to property owners, and Gibbs was among the first to be elected. In a demonstration of the political muscle the Black community could exercise, Gibbs and 17 other Black property owners voted as a block to elect two candidates—George Hunter Cary and Selim Franklin—in the process intentionally defeating Amor de Cosmos, the radical publisher of *The British Colonist*. De Cosmos was a bitter opponent of James Douglas. From the first issues of his newspaper, he had launched a series of harsh attacks against the governor.

The story of de Cosmos is an intriguing part of British Columbia's history. Born William Alexander Smith in New Brunswick, he managed to get an act of the California legislature to change his name to Amor de Cosmos (he later capitalized the "d"), "lover of the universe." He was as eccentric as his name, founding what is now the *Victoria Times Colonist* in 1858. He was briefly a member of the Canadian parliament, the second premier of BC and a lifelong enemy of Sir James Douglas. (Ironically, Douglas and de Cosmos are buried, not more than 200 feet apart, in Victoria's Ross Bay Cemetery.) In a strange turn of events, both Gibbs and de Cosmos were members of an 1867 delegation that worked to bring British Columbia into Confederation.

In 1866, Gibbs, now a British citizen, was elected to the Victoria Town Council and became chairman of the Finance Committee. But in 1869, after spending more

Sir James Douglas lies in an elegant plot in Victoria's Ross Bay Cemetery. Interestingly, his archrival Amor de Cosmos, the second premier of BC, is buried a stone's throw away.

than 10 years north of the border, Gibbs decided it was time to return to the United States. The Civil War had ended, Abraham Lincoln had moved to abolish slavery and conditions for Blacks in the U.S. seemed to be improving. Gibbs' wife, Maria, and their children had left for the States the previous year to join other members of their family. After settling his affairs in what was now Canada, Gibbs moved south. He enrolled in law school at a business college in Oberlin, Ohio, and, in 1871, moved to Little Rock, Arkansas. He spent a year with a local firm then established his own law practice. In subsequent years he held various judicial and political positions and, in 1897, was appointed American Consul to Madagascar. He returned to the United States in 1901 and became president of an African American savings bank in Little Rock.

Gibbs made his last visit to Victoria in 1907. He was honoured in a number of ceremonies for his business acumen and for the dedication that had helped to build a community. Mifflin Wistar Gibbs, a pioneer in the development of British Columbia, died a wealthy man in Little Rock on July 11, 1915.

The influence exercised by Gibbs, Douglas and other members of the Black community in the development of British Columbia lasted only a few years. But their presence critically strengthened James Douglas' hand as he strove to keep the territory in British hands and, ultimately, as part of the Dominion of Canada. By the end of 1858, the Black community had become the majority non-Aboriginal population of Victoria. They founded businesses and participated fully in the life of the community. Some were recruited as members of the colony's first police force. One report has a Jamaican as the first chief of police. Others started farms, and a few tried their hands in the gold fields. In contrast to what had occurred in California, in British Columbia a separate church was not established, people having decided that it was better to become actively involved in existing local churches instead. Reverend Cridge invited them to join his congregation, and many did. The Gibbs and Lester families belonged to the congregation of Reverend Cridge's Christ Church Cathedral.

In 1860, in response to continuing threats from the U.S., members of the Black community offered Governor

The plaque at the foot of Sir James Douglas'grave. His wife, Amelia, and some of his children are buried in the same plot.

James Douglas their services as a volunteer militia. Douglas was concerned, among other things, with what became known as the Pig War. San Juan Island had been used earlier as a Hudson's Bay Company farm but was occupied by U.S. troops after an American settler shot a British pig. Douglas precipitously ordered the British Naval force at Fort Esquimalt to take the island back. But the British commander, Admiral Baynes, refused to start what might have led to outright war with the U.S. The Americans were spoiling for a fight, some itching to take over Vancouver Island. Under the circumstances, Douglas was happy to accept the offer of a self-supporting militia. Cooler heads eventually resolved the Pig War, outright conflict was avoided, and today San Juan Island is on the American side of the border, part of Washington state. In August 2009, the island community celebrated the 150th anniversary of the Peaceful Resolution of the International Boundary Dispute, which took place from June to October 1859.

In July 1861, the Victoria Pioneer Rifle Company, with about 50 Black men partially sponsored by Mifflin Gibbs, was officially sworn in. A "Committee of Coloured Ladies" helped raise money. It is a sobering reflection of the times, however, that when James Douglas retired in 1864, the militia, also known as the African Rifles, was not allowed to participate in his farewell ceremonies. The new governor, Arthur Kennedy, refused to recognize the company and, in the spring of 1865, it disbanded in humiliation and disgust.

For a time, the Black community in Victoria grew and prospered in spite of continued incidents of racism, mostly from Americans passing through to the gold fields. One of the most successful Blacks was John Sullivan Deas, who developed the technology to safely can salmon and played a major role in establishing the British Columbia canning industry. Deas, born in South Carolina in 1838, moved to California in 1860 and to Victoria in 1862, where he established a hardware store at the corner of Fort and Broad streets.

An expert tinsmith, Deas took over a cannery built near New Westminster in 1872 by Captain Edward Stamp. Deas moved the operation to what is now Deas Island, and, by 1874, the cannery was made up of three large buildings occupying a seven-acre site surrounded by a dike. The property included a wharf and several smaller buildings. It was the most successful canning operation in the west. In 1878 Deas sold the business for a reported

$13,000 to $15,000 and moved back to the U.S. With his wife and seven children, he settled in Portland, Oregon. He died on July 22, 1880, at the age of 42.

Some members of the Black community returned to the U.S. after the Civil War ended in 1865, but many remained in Victoria, with others branching out to establish communities in places like Salt Spring Island. At this writing, Nadine Sims, granddaughter of the island's first settlers, Louis and Silvia Stark, was alive and well, a feisty 87-year-old. She is on track to match her grandmother's great age of 105. The Starks first arrived in 1860 with 15 cows, and they established a homestead on 100 acres of land. A great granddaughter still lives on the property.

But as British Columbia attracted more broadly based settlement after it became part of the Dominion of Canada, old patterns of discrimination established themselves. Blacks who had enjoyed unencumbered citizenship in the days before Confederation found themselves excluded from the growing white mainstream. At the same time, many of them intermarried, and their descendents have complexions that are often on the borderline between Black and white.

But there is no denying the critical role that Blacks played in helping James Douglas to keep British Columbia under the British flag.

Two hundred and fifty years before Douglas governed British Columbia, another remarkable individual, Mathieu Da Costa, whose story has almost been obscured by the sands of time, played an important role in opening up the eastern coast to European exploration and settlement.

HERE AT THE BEGINNING

The great changes in world development are occasionally the result of hapless individuals who, by accident or design, foment incidents that change the course of history. Wrong person. Wrong place. Wrong time. But more often than not, change is brought about by leaders who change both perceptions and behaviour through unprecedented achievement, often by overcoming physical, social, political and cultural barriers. They blaze new trails that others can use and expand. The people whose lives are described in this book were and are pioneers. Many of the contributions they have made toward the development of Canada are stirring examples for a more tolerant and democratic society. Much of what follows in this book chronicles and celebrates these accomplishments.

A lot has been written about the barriers of racism. And much more is calling out to be documented. But it is remarkable individuals such as James Douglas, Mifflin Gibbs and the legions of others who opened doors that helped to make Canada one of the best, most peaceable countries in the world. We're far from perfect, of course—that is a necessary disclaimer. But to paraphrase Sir Winston Churchill, we have the worst system in the world—except, of course, for all of the others.

The first Black to have played a positive role in the development of what was to become Canada was Mathieu Da Costa, a multilingual explorer, navigator, interpreter and guide who, in the early 1600s, facilitated trade and communications between the early explorer Samuel de Champlain and the First Nations people of what is now Nova Scotia. Some records tell us that Da Costa's African birth name might have been Lusofonia, the name Da Costa (sometimes recorded as "de Costa" or "d'Acosta") having been acquired from the Portuguese who were among the earliest explorers both of west Africa and North America.

It's possible that, like James Douglas, Da Costa was the child of a mixed union between a European father and an African mother—not an unusual occurrence during the early days of exploration when, as early as the 1400s, many Europeans settled on the Africa coast. His birth date is lost, but he is known to have died in 1623. He is the first recorded free Black in Canadian history. What we know about him is based on the few records that historians have uncovered. We don't know what he looked like as there is no portrait of him. A drawing, apparently made long after his passing, imagines his appearance. The image depicts a dapper, narrow-faced man with a neatly trimmed beard. He wears a tailored suit and a broad-brimmed hat sporting a feather.

Da Costa was a freeman who must have travelled to North America, possibly with Portuguese fishermen during the late 1500s, learning a number of Native languages in the process. Some sources suggest that there may have been similarities between African and North American indigenous languages that made communication easier. In addition to Mi'kmaq, he was said to be fluent in Portuguese, Dutch, English and French as well as a pidgin version of Basque, which was for a time the lingua franca used for trading purposes between Europeans and North American Natives. Records show that in about 1605 he was a member of a party led by a French nobleman Pierre Du Gua de Monts and Samuel de Champlain. Da Costa worked with explorers and traders from a number of countries before taking on the role of guide and interpreter for Champlain.

In 1608, Da Costa signed a contract in Amsterdam that committed him to sail with or on behalf of Du Gua as an interpreter "pour les voyages de Canada," to take effect in January 1609 and to last for three years. The annual salary was 60 crowns (about 195 livres), a significant amount at that time. Another story suggests that a Rouen merchant kidnapped Da Costa and sold or loaned him to Du Gua as an interpreter.

French newspapers reported that, in 1608, Da Costa was working for the government of Port Royal on the north shore of present-day Annapolis Basin, a sheltered bay on the south shore of the Bay of Fundy. The new settlement was founded by Du Gua de Monts, Samuel de Champlain, Louis Hebért and Sieur de Poutrincourt after they spent a disastrous winter trying to settle on Ile Saint-Croix.

Another source has Da Costa imprisoned in Le Havre in December 1609. The mention of "insolences" suggests that in addition to being remarkably mobile, he was independent, proud and probably quite self-possessed. We can imagine Da Costa as a strong, healthy adventurer with a quick intelligence and an easy capacity to learn languages. He was a good negotiator who knew the value of money and probably accumulated some wealth. In the mainstream history of the Western world, Mathieu Da Costa is an asterisk. But his presence indicates that Blacks were very much a part of the development of the New World. It's unlikely that he was the only African involved in the early exploration of North America. A tradition that saw Europeans engaging African interpreters and explorers had its beginnings in the late 15th or early 16th century.

Da Costa is commemorated at the Port Royal National Historic Site at Annapolis Royal, Nova Scotia. His name stands beside those intrepid adventurers who set the stage for this remarkable country. In May 2004, a private member's bill in the Canadian Parliament called for the establishment of the first Monday in February as Mathieu Da Costa Day. The bill died on the order paper but was re-introduced in the House of Commons by MP Marlene Jennings in January 29, 2005, and, at this writing, is still before the House.

Almost 175 years after Da Costa's exploits in the New World, a mass migration from the United States led to the creation of the first substantial Black community in Canada. The "Book of Negroes" is an actual handwritten document that records the names of the some 3000 Blacks who sailed from New York to Nova Scotia between April 23 and November 30, 1783, with the United Empire Loyalists. There are three copies: one at the Public Records Office in Kew, England; one at the National Archives in Washington, DC; and one at the Nova Scotia Archives in Halifax. In today's digital world, the document is available online. *The Book of Negroes* is also the title of a novel written by the celebrated writer Lawrence Hill. The award-winning novel takes you into the imagined life of a former slave who was part of that migration. It gives poignant, richly detailed insights into what life was like for the Black Loyalists of Nova Scotia.

In real life, Black Nova Scotians faced unexpected hardships. The promised land delivered much less than it had offered. But individuals such as Rose Fortune and Carrie Best, who lived in different generations of the communities that grew up in and around Halifax, rose above the restrictions they faced to set examples of how courage and determination can overcome substantial odds.

ROSE FORTUNE

The Fortune name appears several times in the "Book of Negroes." And one of those names, Rose Fortune, is an almost mythical figure. She had an inauspicious beginning, born into slavery in Virginia, reportedly the property of a family named Devone. Yet she grew up to be one of the most incredible characters in Canadian history. I describe her as incredible, because, if I made her up, most people would not believe such a person existed.

A more definitive record of the Fortune name is seen on the muster roll of Loyalists at Annapolis in June 1784. It contains a record of "Fortune—a free Negro," who appears on the list with his wife and a "child above ten." These two excerpts from the muster roll of discharged officers, disbanded soldiers and Loyalists taken in Annapolis County from June 18 to 24, 1784, almost certainly refers to the family of Rose Fortune (ca. 1774–1864). A careful comparison of the digital version with the actual transcript shows that the headers for the columns "children above ten" and "children under ten" have been reversed. This was the result of an error made, on that page only, when the original muster roll was transcribed in the 19th century.

Little is known about Rose's parents or if she had any siblings. The Nova Scotia census for 1838, which lists only heads of households, makes no reference to Rose Fortune. But we know that the Fortunes settled in Annapolis Royal where Mathieu Da Costa had worked some 175 years earlier.

Details of her early life in Annapolis Royal are sparse. Despite extensive documentation for a number of other Black Loyalists of her generation in the St. Luke's Church of England records, there is no mention at all of her parents, and the only official record of Rose is her burial. There are no baptismal records for her three children, although their own marriages are recorded in St. Luke's register. It's not inconceivable that Rose Fortune had an aversion to official records.

An Internet search will turn up a watercolour drawing of a short, forward-leaning woman, that, although the artist is unknown, was probably taken from life. Her profile depicts a stocky woman with a determined jaw. She wears workman's boots and a man's overcoat over what looks like a heavy dress. An apron hangs down below the three-quarter-length coat, and a petticoat protrudes beneath her below-the-knees dress. She wears a straw hat over what appears to be a lace kerchief or cap. Her arm is crooked through a straw basket, and she wears white gloves. The picture is sometimes reproduced with her facing right; other times it shows her facing left. Either way, it presents a picture of someone you wouldn't want to pick a fight with. She is reported to have carried a short but substantial stick that she did not hesitate to use.

This tough, diminutive woman became a leading citizen of Annapolis Royal, was the community's first police officer and founded a business that her descendents carried on for 100 years. As a young woman having to earn a living, Rose Fortune acquired a wheelbarrow and began carting luggage between ships arriving at the dock and local hotels. She made collections and deliveries, helped travellers find better accommodation and offered a wake-up service for people who had to get up in time for business appointments or for sailings of the Saint John-Digby-Annapolis ferry. She protected her business vigorously; any boys attempting to infringe upon her monopoly were likely to become acquainted with her stick.

Many Canadians will remember growing up in small communities at a time when it seemed that all adults assumed responsibility for the disciplining of local children. If a kid got into mischief, he or she was dealt with on the spot by whatever adult was handy; if you didn't get a spanking or a good swat, your mother was sure to know what you had done before you got home. "Spare the rod and spoil the child" was the operative maxim for proper childrearing. Rose Fortune took on the role of parent-at-large in Annapolis Royal and soon became the community's unofficial police officer, keeping unruly youngsters and adults in order. She imposed and enforced curfews on the wharves and in the surrounding areas, ordering people home if they had no business being out.

Rose Fortune, one of the most forceful personalities you could encounter, was on familiar terms with leading citizens and seems, literally, to have known everybody. And everyone knew who she was. Although she never wore a badge, her authority as a police presence was recognized.

There's an interesting report of an encounter written in 1852 by a Lieutenant-Colonel Sleigh of the 77th Regiment:

> I was aided in my hasty efforts to quit the abominable Inn by a curious old Negro woman, rather stunted in growth…and dressed in a man's coat and felt hat; she had a small stick in her hand which she applied lustily to the backs of all who did not jump instantly out of the way. Poor old dame! She was evidently a privileged character.

Rose replaced her wheelbarrow with horse-drawn wagons, and her business prospered. Although she had at least three children, she may not have married. She was always known by the name of Fortune, and her off-spring carried her surname. Their marriages, however, are recognized in church records. Jane Fortune married Isaac Godfrey, son of Black Loyalist Edward Godfrey, on December 21, 1830. Isaac and Jane Godfrey are buried in the Garrison Cemetery at Fort Anne. Their tombstones stand near the entrance to the Court House. Rose's final resting place is probably nearby, though her grave is unmarked. It may not be a stretch to surmise that Rose Fortune was as tough and independent in her relationship with the church as she was with others in her life. If she had children out of wedlock or lived in a relationship not sanctioned by the church, she may well have been denied full rites at her passing.

John Fortune married Isaac's sister Hester Godfrey, on January 13, 1838. And Margaret Fortune married John Francis of Digby. A granddaughter, Charlotte Amazie Francis, married Albert Lewis of Annapolis Royal and had 12 children. After Rose's death, Lewis carried on the business she had founded. By the 1870s, his mother-in-law's baggage-handling business had grown to include coaches and wagons that were always on hand to transport passengers and freight to and from the railway station, the wharves and the hotels. After Albert's death in 1882, his son, James, carried on the business as James Lewis & Son. A grandson, James Lewis Jr., bought the firm's first truck. As Lewis Transfer, the company survived as a Black-owned business until the death of James Lewis in 1960.

Rose is said to have suffered from rheumatism in her later years but continued to work until well into her 70s, reportedly living near the Union Bank, now the Royal Bank of Canada. Her death is recorded among the burials at St. Luke's Church of England, Annapolis Royal, on February 20, 1867: "age unknown, supposed about ninety."

Long after her death, Rose was remembered as one of the most remarkable citizens of early Annapolis Royal. On July 19, 2008, a special ceremony was held to celebrate the unveiling of the Rose Fortune Interpretive Panel adjacent to the Fort Anne National Historic Site in Annapolis Royal. Developed by the Valley African Nova Scotian Development Association, the project received funding from federal, provincial and municipal governments, as well as from the Halifax-based Black Business Initiative.

Rose Fortune is recognized today by the Association of Black Law Enforcers of Canada as the first Black policewoman in Canada, perhaps in North America. The association has created a scholarship in her name. Her life is celebrated annually on March 13.

The descendants of extraordinary people often achieve extraordinary things. In 1984 Daurene Lewis, seven generations removed from her ancestor Rose Fortune, was elected mayor of Annapolis Royal, the first Black female mayor in North America. A Dalhousie University graduate, she has advanced degrees in nursing, an MBA from Saint Mary's University and an honorary doctorate from Mount Saint Vincent University.

CARRIE BEST

There is no discernable family connection between Carrie Best and Rose Fortune, the incredible character who became Annapolis' first police officer and founded a business that lasted 100 years. But a righteous link connects these incomparable women. Both were fearless in their unerring pursuit of justice, both lived long lives, both made their own opportunities and challenged adversity everywhere it confronted them. Best is surely a spiritual descendent of Rose Fortune.

Carrie Best, child of a new era, had somewhat different beginnings. While she didn't begin life in slavery, as Rose Fortune had done, she nevertheless grew up in a world in which legally sanctioned discrimination against Blacks was the norm. Carrie was born at the dawn of the 20th century, on March 4, 1903, in New Glasgow, Nova Scotia. Her father, James Ashe Prevoe, was a labourer; her mother, Georgina, was a cook for white families, including a local judge. Educational segregation was the law, and women were limited to "domestic" work. Georgina was a courageous fighter who fought for her children. In her 1977 autobiography, *That Lonesome Road,* Carrie Best tells the story of how her mother walked into the heart of an excited mob to rescue her son. World War I was winding down when an interracial clash in New Glasgow led to a race riot that saw bands of weapon-brandishing white youth blocking the entry of Blacks into parts of the city. Carrie's older brother was trapped in a hotel behind the lines:

> ...as my mother drew near they hurled insults at her and threateningly ordered her to turn back. She continued to walk toward the hotel about a block away when one of the young men recognized her and asked her where she was going. "I am going to the Norfolk House for my son," she answered calmly. (My mother was six feet tall and straight as a ramrod.) The young man ordered the crowd back and my mother continued on her way to the hotel...my mother found my frightened older brother and brought him safely home.

Carrie showed signs of a superior intelligence as a child. She was four years old when she wrote her first poem, the prelude to a lifelong devotion to literature. After she graduated from high school, her parents somehow mustered the resources to send her to school in Chicago to study nursing and teaching. It seems that neither profession suited her; she probably decided that she would not fit comfortably into the stereotypes that came with the only professions generally open to women. Her strong-willed mother told her to "Take the first turn right and go straight ahead" to find her own destiny.

Carrie Prevoe came home from school in Chicago and, in 1925, married Albert Best, a railway porter. In those days, working on the railroad was one of the few jobs that allowed a Black man to earn a decent living. The practice of hiring Blacks to work as porters was begun by the American Pullman Railroad company and quickly adopted by Canadian railroads. It was the only job reserved exclusively for Black men, and while they suffered both institutionalized discrimination and daily racial insults, their jobs were relatively secure. Although they had exclusive access to work as porters, no other railroad jobs were open to them.

Porters were expected to attend to every wish of their often mean-spirited passengers. But through the Dirty Thirties, railway porters were much better off than the hordes of unemployed whites who roamed the country, many, ironically, riding the rails. Porters, "on the road" for much of the time, were nevertheless pillars in their communities and gave their families a great deal of financial stability. Albert's job provided Carrie with the security to pursue her own interests. The couple had a son named Calbert, a composite of their names, and later adopted two girls.

Carrie, inspired by her mother's deep-seated antipathy to injustice, soon became involved in human rights issues. When Black families needed help to pay their taxes, Carrie gave poetry readings to help raise money. She became a prolific writer of letters to the editor of various newspapers.

By 1946, she decided that letters to the editor were not enough; too many stories affecting the Black community were not being reported. An incident that surely convinced Best of the need for a place for stories the mainstream media wouldn't touch occurred when she and her son, Cal, were arrested for sitting in the "white" section of the Roseland Theatre. They refused to move and were fined for disturbing the peace. So in July 1946, she and Calbert launched *The Clarion,* the first Black newspaper in Nova Scotia. The first issue was an 8"×10" one-page bulletin distributed through churches. Its mission was to be both a voice and a source of information for the Black community and to promote interracial understanding and goodwill.

Within a year, Carrie incorporated Clarion Publishing Company and, with backing from prominent leaders of the white community, such as Lemuel B. Mills, a New Glasgow contractor, and Dr. A. Waddell, a Halifax physician, was producing a weekly broadsheet newspaper. She filled the newspaper with reports of racial issues. She checked stores, restaurants and hotels and reported on how they treated Black customers. A persistent investigative reporter, she blew the whistle on scams and injustices. In one case, she discovered a scam in which Black property owners were forced to pay higher taxes in order to coerce them to sell. With support from the provincial premier, she prepared a report for the Human Rights Commission.

The December 1946 issue of *The Clarion* headlined the story of Viola Desmond, a successful beautician and teacher who got caught in an incident that echoed Carrie's earlier movie theatre experience. On November 8, while travelling to Sidney, Desmond's car broke down in New Glasgow. She was told that it could not be repaired until the next day, so she decided to overnight in New Glasgow. To pass the time, she went to a movie at the same Roseland Theatre and asked for a main floor seat. The teller gave her a ticket to the balcony, where, although there were no signs that said so, Blacks were supposed to sit. Desmond insisted on sitting on the main floor. An usher ordered her to move. She offered to pay the price difference between the balcony and the main floor seats but was refused. Desmond stayed put. The manager called the police, who forcefully removed her, injuring her knee and her hip. She spent the next 12 hours in jail, and somewhere along the way her purse disappeared. She was charged with refusing to pay the tax on the higher-priced main floor seats. A local judge sentenced her to 30 days in jail for tax evasion and imposed a $20 fine.

The recently formed Nova Scotia Association for the Advancement of Coloured People raised the money to pay the fine and legal fees. The case was appealed all the way to the Nova Scotia Supreme Court. Carrie Best travelled to Halifax to cover and report on the trial. Appeals to overturn the sentence failed. The judges ruled that no error in law had taken place. Desmond had refused to stay in the place assigned to her by the mainstream community. There's little doubt that many Blacks, before and after Viola Desmond, ran afoul of the law of segregation in theatres. *The Clarion* made the case a cause célèbre. It was not until 1954 that Nova Scotia repealed its segregation laws. But the Viola Desmond story became one of the most publicized cases of racial discrimination in the era.

The Clarion was published until 1956, chronicling a decade that saw the beginning of a slow rise to acceptance by Nova Scotia's Black community. Carrie Best moved on, writing articles for the *Halifax Herald* and the *Nova Scotia Gleaner.* In 1968 she was hired to write a regular column for the *Pictou Advocate* under the heading of Human Rights. The column ran until 1975.

One of Best's most satisfying pursuits was a Sunday radio program, *The Quiet Corner*, launched in 1952. She read literature and poetry against a backdrop of mostly classical music. The show, heard on four or five radio stations, aired for 12 years. At the same time, she managed a busy timetable as a speaker and advocate, among other things founding the Kay Livingstone Visible Minority Women's Society of Nova Scotia in 1975. She intervened in a public hearing on the Donald Marshall case, making a passionate defence of the wrongly convicted Mi'kmaq hero. One observer, Aboriginal leader Daniel Paul, described Best as "a true warrior in the ongoing struggle to defeat racism and other forms of intolerance. Her message came straight from the heart."

In 1977 she published her autobiography, *That Lonesome Road,* which she described as the "reminiscences of a journey into identity." That same year, with Carrie in her mid-70s, *The Clarion* saw a brief revival as *The Negro Citizen.* Part of its purpose was to publicize her side of an issue involving a land dispute.

Carrie Best, whose life spanned the 20th century, was well recognized with many awards. She was inducted into the Order of Canada in 1974 and, five years later, was elevated to the status of Officer within the Order. She was awarded honorary doctorates by both Dalhousie University and the University of Kings College in Halifax. She continued to be active until her death at the age of 98 on July 24, 2001.

CHAPTER THREE

CHANGING PERCEPTIONS IN UPPER CANADA

JOSIAH HENSON

While Rose Fortune was keeping the peace in Annapolis Royal, a fiercely determined man was making his way up the Underground Railway to Canada. His youth well behind him, Josiah Henson was already 40 when he crossed the border with his family in 1830 into what was then the Province of Upper Canada.

Photos of Henson taken later in his life reveal a man with a strong, distinguished character; his well-proportioned head is framed by an abundance of white hair and a trimmed beard. Over a broad African nose, his eyes look thought-fully into the middle distance, as though he is contem-plating a response to a particularly interesting question. His picture was featured on a Canadian stamp in 1999, the first Black man in Canada to be commemorated on a postage stamp. Jazz piano giant Oscar Peterson was commemorated on a 2005 stamp, and in 2009,

Canada Post issued stamps honouring Rosemary Brown and Abraham Shadd.

Henson's name might ring a tiny bell with some mainstream Canadians—something about *Uncle Tom's Cabin* and the Underground Railway. But few know of the impact Henson had on the development of the country that adopted him. He was the founder of a self-sustaining Black community in southern Ontario. The lumber industry he created took him to the first World's Fair, held in London, England, in 1851–52. Queen Victoria came to see his wares and, when he returned to England years later, she invited him to dinner. He was hosted by the British prime minister, Lord John Russell, and became friends with John Whitgift, the Archbishop of Canterbury.

When the archbishop, impressed by Henson's informed grasp of world affairs, asked him what university he had attended, Henson replied, "the University of Adversity." His autobiography, *The Life of Josiah Henson, Formerly a Slave, Now an Inhabitant of Canada, as Narrated by Himself* (1849), reveals a formidable and articulate intelligence. It is, even today, a highly readable and literate document—amazing for a man who didn't learn to read until well into adult life. Henson was an inspiring preacher and a truly gifted human who, in today's world, would likely have risen to high political office.

Josiah Henson was born on June 15, 1789, in Port Tobacco, Charles County, Maryland. In the practice of the times, he was given the Christian name of his owner, Dr. Josiah McPherson. Henson was the surname of his master's uncle. Henson spent the first 40 years of his life as a slave, and on one occasion he was beaten so badly that his right arm and shoulder blade were broken. He was never again able to raise that arm above his head. Henson discovered Christianity when he was 18, and it changed his life. By 1828 he was a part-time preacher for the Methodist Episcopal Church, gifted enough to earn money from his sermons.

The high principles he adopted made him both loyal and scrupulously honest; he was so forgiving of the soul-destroying treatment that his masters rained down on him and fellow slaves that he passed up early opportunities to escape. It was only after his owner brazenly cheated him out of the $350 he had spent years saving to buy his freedom that he concluded that his only acceptable future was to run away to Canada.

The harrowing journey began in the summer of 1830. The family hid in the woods by day and cautiously travelled by night. Henson and his wife, Charlotte, a fellow slave he had married in 1811 when he was 22, had four children at that time. Two were so young that he had to carry them strapped to his back. The family, travelling on their own, suffered sickness, were sometimes threatened by wolves and came close to starvation. Finding food and water where they could, they were on constant alert for any encounter with whites who would surely have sent them back to their former owners or worse. The exceptions were a band of Natives, who at one point literally saved the family from starvation, and the Quakers, who courageously assisted Blacks travelling the then-established Underground Railway.

From the point of their escape in Kentucky, the Henson family travelled through Cincinnati, Buffalo and New York, and after nearly four months, finally set foot on Canadian soil on October 28, 1830, eventually settling near Colchester in southern Ontario. Henson's first home was a shack that had been inhabited by pigs. The family cleaned the place out and established, for the first time, a home of their own in which they could enjoy "some of the comforts of life, while the necessities of food and fuel were abundant."

By the time Henson reached Canada, there was already a growing population of Blacks in southern Ontario. Few had land of their own, with most working as labourers or sharecroppers on white-owned farms. Henson worked as a farm labourer for his first three or four years in Canada, while at the same time serving as a preacher for the area's Black community. He asked his oldest son, then 12, to teach him to read and write. He quickly became involved in helping others who had followed his path, becoming a conductor on the Underground Railway. He slipped back across the border into the U.S. several times and led more than 200 slaves to freedom in Canada. His qualities of leadership fully developed, he was the captain of a troop of Black volunteers during the Upper Canadian Rebellion of 1837–38.

Henson and an associate, Hiram Wilson, had met a few years earlier and were able to rent government land and set the stage for the creation of a viable Black community named Dawn. In 1842 they bought 200 acres at a cost of $800 that became the site for Dawn. With the purchase of additional property, the area grew to some 500 residents. The American Anti-Slavery Society and a group of Boston Unitarians supported Dawn in its creation of the British-American Institute, the first school for Blacks. The school taught agricultural and industrial skills to former slaves, encouraging them to buy their own property. Henson states in his autobiography, "We look to the school, and the possession of landed property by individuals, as the two great means of elevation of our oppressed and degraded race."

During the same year, Henson was in a position to purchase his own land, 200 acres near what is now

Dresden, Ontario. The property contained stands of black walnut trees, and Henson soon established a business exporting the highly desirable lumber to Boston and New York. His homestead still stands and is a popular tourist attraction.

The man who only learned to read and write in his 40s published the first edition of his biography in 1849. It was reprinted in 1858 as *Truth Stranger than Fiction: Father Henson's Story of his Own Life,* with an introduction by the abolitionist Harriet Beecher Stowe. A third edition, entitled *Truth Stranger than Fiction; An Autobiography of the Rev. Josiah Henson,* appeared in 1879.

Henson's story is the stuff of legend; it became the inspiration for the famous *Uncle Tom's Cabin,* written by Stowe in 1952. According to some reports, Henson had met Mrs. Stowe when he was passing through Maine on an anti-slavery preaching tour. The two became friends, and as she learned the details of his life, she wrote *Uncle Tom's Cabin,* with Henson as the model for the novel's protagonist. The book became the second bestselling book (after the Bible) of the 19th century. At one point, as many as five stage versions of the book played in London, England. According to Wikipedia, in the first year after the book was published, 300,000 copies were sold in the United States alone. The book's impact was so great that when Abraham Lincoln met Stowe at the start of the Civil War, he is often quoted as having declared, "So this is the little lady who made this big war."

Some reviewers, particularly from the American south, challenged the book's authenticity, angrily arguing that the lot of slaves could not have been as bad as portrayed. In response, Stowe wrote a second book, *A Key to Uncle Tom's Cabin,* in which she documented the stories of actual slaves who were the basis for the fictional characters she created. Henson, who had become an active anti-slavery preacher, referred to himself as the "real" Uncle Tom during his lecture tours. One source quotes Henson as saying "Mrs Stowe's book is not an exaggerated account of the evils of slavery. The truth has never been half told; the story would be too horrible to hear." As a boy, Henson watched as his father had his ear nailed to a post and then cut off following a beating of 100 lashes. His crime? He was trying to prevent a white overseer from raping his wife. His father was then literally "sold down the river" to another slaver in the Deep South. Josiah never saw him again.

In 1852, now a successful entrepreneur, Henson took samples of his wood products to exhibit at the Great Exhibition of the Works of Industry of All Nations, the World's Fair held in Hyde Park, London. The London fair was the first World's Fair, the largest event of its kind ever held, attended by more than six million people. Henson was the only Black exhibitor. Representing Canada, he won a bronze medal for the craftsmanship of his exhibit, which included sheets of black walnut polished to mirror smoothness.

At the age of 87, Henson, now an international celebrity, returned to England in 1876 to attend another World's Fair. This time, Queen Victoria, who had visited his exhibit during the first World's Fair, invited him to a special audience and presented him with a gold-framed photograph of herself. His signature is in the visitor's book at Windsor Castle. To commemorate the meeting, the artist Francis Walker painted a watercolour. A bust of Henson made by W. Charles May is on exhibit at the American Museum in Britain, at Claverton Manor in Bath.

Josiah Henson, a natural leader, led a full and note-worthy life. He died at his home in Dresden, Ontario, on May 5, 1883, at the age of 94. The state of his birth, Maryland, named a park after him in 1991. In Canada, Henson is recognized as a Canadian of National Historical Significance. And, there's the stamp. Henson was an unofficial international ambassador for the country that adopted him.

MARY ANN SHADD CARY

As the Underground Railway brought tens of thousands of American Blacks to freedom in Canada, crusaders brought different approaches to consolidate their establishment in their new country. (Various sources suggest that between 30,000 and 60,000 slaves came to Canada during the most active phase of the migration, between 1810 and 1850. The lower estimate is probably more realistic.) Canada, under the leadership of John Simcoe, had abolished slavery in 1833, and the prospect of being able to vote, to own property and to participate in civic affairs was like the pull of a magnet. Across the border, the Fugitive Slave Law, passed in 1850, acted like the opposite pole of the magnet and pushed thousands northward.

While Josiah Henson was influencing developments around Dawn, Mary Ann Shadd, settling a few kilometres to the south in Chatham, had a different view of how Black immigrants should fit into Canadian society.

Born Mary Ann Camberton Shadd in Wilmington, Delaware, on October 9, 1823, Mary Ann was the oldest of 13 children born to Abraham and Harriett Shadd. Her father was the son of Hans Schad (the name was Americanized to "Shadd"), a former German soldier, and a free Black woman, Elizabeth Jackson. Schad operated a successful shoemaker business that Abraham later adopted.

Mary Ann's childhood home was a station on the Underground Railway. She saw her father play a key role as a "conductor," helping escaped slaves travel up the line, and she developed a keen understanding of the racism and social issues of the time early in her life. When her family moved to Chester, Pennsylvania, Mary Ann was enrolled at a school operated by a Quaker society, where she received a solid education. Having completed her education at 16, Mary Ann moved back to Wilmington and opened a school for Blacks. She was no doubt influenced by her father's strong beliefs and her highly moral Quaker education. She was familiar with the American Moral Reform Society, an organization to which her father belonged and whose mandate called for the abolition of slavery and endorsed universal fellowship as opposed to individual racial identities.

Mary Ann Shadd fled to Canada in 1851 when the U.S. Fugitive Slave Law opened the door for bounty hunters to legally capture both escaped slaves and free Blacks anywhere they could find them. She was 27 when she and a younger brother, Isaac, moved to Windsor. Her family followed her in 1853, moving into the North Buxton area of southern Ontario.

The town of Buxton, 19 kilometres south of present-day Chatham, was a major Canadian terminal of the Underground Railway. The community was founded with the help of Reverend William King, a Presbyterian minister from Londonderry, Ireland, who migrated to Louisiana and, through marriage, found himself to be the owner of 15 slaves. A dedicated abolitionist, the idea of slavery was abhorrent to him, and he moved the slaves and his family to Canada. He gave the slaves freedom at Buxton, which became the country's largest planned fugitive slave community.

Buxton's St. Andrews Church was graced by the now-famous Liberty Bell, which hangs in the steeple and calls the faithful to worship to this day. The 258-kilogram bell was commissioned by a Pittsburgh physician, Martin Delaney. According to the inscription, the bell was presented "by the Coloured inhabitants of Pittsburgh" to the inhabitants of the Elgin settlement, also known as Buxton, as a "lasting memorial." The bell was rung every time a slave reached freedom in Canada. A replica of the bell is on display at Buxton Museum.

Quickly involving himself in community affairs as a leader, in 1858, Abraham Shadd became the first Black man elected as a councillor of Raleigh Township.

With support from the American Missionary Association, Mary Ann soon established a racially integrated school in Windsor. It was an act that defined her contribution to the development of Black society in Canada, but it also put her at odds with Josiah Henson and many others who, with the experience of slavery still resonating in their souls, favoured separate schools. The thought of integration with the dominant white society was too great a leap of faith for people whose bodies still bore the scars of slavery.

One of the strongest supporters of keeping Blacks in their own community was Henry Bibb, a leader in the Black community in Windsor and a powerful newspaper publisher. He used his publication, *The Voice of the Fugitive,* to attack both Shadd's character and her position. Their rivalry was bitter and hard fought; Shadd hit back with equal vitriol, often attacking Josiah Henson himself. With the help a former slave, newspaper editor and Congregational minister, Samuel Ringgold Ward, Shadd founded her own newspaper in 1853. The *Provincial Freeman* was "devoted to anti-slavery, temperance and general literature." The battle was on. The first iteration of the newspaper did not last long, but Shadd soon reincarnated it from premises on Toronto's King Street and continued its publication for another five years.

The paper became a champion of temperance, civil rights and Black self-determination, which, in her view, included equality and integration for Blacks. She argued that separate churches, schools and communities were counter-productive and would undermine the long-term freedom of her people. In the end, her beliefs seem to have prevailed. Many of the Blacks who moved to southern Ontario via the Underground Railway appear to have blended in with the white population, quite a different situation from that in Nova Scotia, where the Black community remained largely separate and distinct.

Eloquent, articulate and considered attractive, partly because of her light skin, Shadd led a public life. In addition to her writing, she championed campaigns to abolish slavery, developing a reputation as a powerful speaker. In 1856, at the age of 32, she married Thomas F. Cary, a Toronto businessman who owned and operated a barbershop. Some observers believed Shadd had wed to escape the taint of being labelled an "old maid" and to increase her respectability. It was an unusual marriage for a woman whose great, great grandniece described her as an early feminist. The marriage certainly did not curtail Shadd's crusading activities—five days after the wedding, she reportedly left on a fundraising trip. She continued writing, went on speaking tours and played an active role in stopping slave catchers who came into Canada hoping to grab fugitive slaves. Later in life she joined the Woman's Suffrage Association in the U.S., working alongside Susan B. Anthony and Elizabeth Cady Stanton to fight for women's suffrage.

Mary Ann moved to Chatham in 1856, soon after her marriage. Her husband joined her two years later, and once settled, the couple had two children. Mary Ann continued to publish the *Provincial Freeman* and to teach school. Descendants of the family still live in southern Ontario. Mary Ann's great, great grandniece, Adrienne Shadd, participated in *Hymn to Freedom,* a four-hour documentary series about the history of Blacks in Canada produced by musician, historian and producer Almeta Speaks. I met Adrienne on the campus of her alma mater, the University of Toronto.

Adrienne Shadd, great, great grandniece of pioneer publisher Mary Ann Shadd—the first black woman to publish a newspaper in North America

Our conversation took place on a warm, sunny spring day, sitting on a park bench on the U of T's famous Philosopher's Walk. Adrienne, who teaches at Ryerson University, told me that she didn't learn about her famous ancestor until she was almost an adult. She started to research her own family history and ultimately the history of Blacks in Ontario because she was dissatisfied with what she had been taught about Black history. Her parents and grandparents, she said, were reluctant to talk about their pioneer ancestors. It's not unusual. Many minority people want to leave the difficulties of the past behind them in order to blend in.

An attractive and fashionably dressed young woman, Adrienne is an author, curator and editor with a number of books in print, including *The Underground Railroad—Next Stop Toronto,* written with Afua Cooper and Karolyn Smardz Frost, and *Talking About Identity,* which she edited with Carl James.

Mary Ann Shadd, she said, was an early feminist and the first woman to publish and edit a newspaper in Canada, and, so far as she knew, the first Black woman to do so in all of North America. Her eyes flashing, she declared that her ancestor was "a woman ahead of her time."

Thomas Cary died in 1860, just before the birth of the couple's second child, Linton. A daughter, Sarah, was three years old, and Mary Ann also cared for three teenaged children from her husband's first marriage. Abraham Lincoln had become president of the United States and had launched the Emancipation Proclamation of 1862, the first step toward the abolition of slavery. American Blacks had found a champion.

On a wave of hope, Mary Ann and her children moved back to the States. During the ensuing Civil War, she helped recruit Black volunteers for the Union

Army and returned to teaching. The family moved to Washington, DC.

In 1869 she enrolled at the Howard University Law School, becoming the first Black woman to enter law school in the United States. She was not, however, the first to graduate. Some reports suggest that illness and the challenges of raising and supporting a young family delayed her passage through university. She did not graduate until 1883, at the age of 60, but did practice law in Washington for a few years.

Mary Ann Shadd died on June 5, 1893, predeceased by her son, Linton. Her daughter, Sarah, in an essay published in *Homespun Heroines and Other Women of Distinction,* recalled an incident that dramatically sums up Shadd's determined and fiery personality.

> One Sunday a slave boy…was overtaken in Chatham and about to be carried off. Mrs. Cary tore the boy from the slave hunters, ran to the court-house and had the bell rung so violently that the whole town was soon aroused. Mrs. Cary with her commanding form, piercing eyes, and stirring voice soon had the people as indignant as herself—denouncing in no uncertain terms the outrage perpetrated under the British flag and demanded that these man-hunters be driven from their midst. The result was that the pursuers fled…

The story stands as a fitting epitaph to Mary Ann's legacy. In 1976, her house in Washington was declared a national historic landmark. There is a plaque, erected in Chatham by the Ontario Historical Foundation on February 21, 1995, that reads:

MARY ANN SHADD CARY 1823–1893

African Americans came to Canada in increasing numbers after the United States passed the Fugitive Slave Act in 1850. Some settled in segregated communities; others, like Mary Ann Shadd, promoted full integration into society. A teacher and anti-slavery crusader, Shadd immigrated to Windsor in 1851. She started the "Provincial Freeman" in 1853 to encourage Blacks to seek equality through education and self-reliance. Two years later she moved the newspaper to Chatham, where it operated for the rest of the decade. Widowed in 1860, Shadd Cary returned to the U.S. in 1863 to work for racial equality in the aftermath of emancipation. She was the first Black woman known to have edited a North American newspaper.

CHAPTER FOUR

HOMESTEADING ON THE PRAIRIES

B lack immigration to Canada's prairies is a story of perseverance. We can only speculate how different this country might be if the Ottawa government had opened its doors in the same way that Upper Canada had done when it received the desperate passengers who fled to freedom up the Underground Railway. In the 20th century, the Canadian government's approach to Black immigration was a far cry from that of Great Britain, which endorsed James Douglas' 1858 invitation to American Blacks to settle in Victoria, arguably saving British Columbia for Canada in the process.

In the early 1900s, as in the late 1850s, the challenge was to put settlers on the land. Douglas needed to reinforce the Empire's ownership of British Columbia. The still relatively new Canadian government needed to reinforce its claim to the prairies. There was a palpable fear that Americans flooding the western United States would stream across the undefended border to take up unoccupied territory in Saskatchewan and Alberta.

Prime Minister John A. Macdonald had invested substantial political and monetary capital in the railway that brought the west coast Crown Colony into Confederation. By the time Sir Wilfrid Laurier was elected to office in 1896, the country faced a desperate need to fill up the wide-open spaces between Ontario and British Columbia. The Canadian Pacific Railway (CPR) needed the business, and the land needed to be occupied. Canada wanted what Sir Clifford Sifton, minister of the interior from 1896 to 1905, characterized as "a stalwart peasant in a sheepskin coat, born on the soil, whose forefathers have been farmers for ten generations, and a stout wife and a half-dozen children." Thousands of them. Sifton's highly romanticized advertising campaigns ultimately resulted in a large influx of Ukrainians, Doukhabors and other eastern Europeans from the remains of the old Austro-Hungarian Empire. The campaign proclaimed, "There is no greater grain growing district in the world than the three prairie provinces."

Canada also advertised in newspapers and pamphlets south of the border, with a particular focus on Oklahoma where available land for people with farming and homesteading experience was fast disappearing. The flatlands of Manitoba, Saskatchewan and Alberta, the pamphlets said, were the "Last, Best West." Canada promised religious freedom and no conscription.

Laurier had established an open-door policy for immigrants from Europe and the United States. But the policy did not apply to everybody. The wives, children and other family members of Chinese workers stranded in Canada were subject to a head tax that rose from $50 to $500. The CPR failed to provide passage home after the

Chinese workers had completed the backbreaking work of building the railroad through the Rockies. The workers had sent home the bulk of their meagre earnings to support their families in China.

In the U.S., many Blacks had moved to Oklahoma in search of freedom. Before becoming a state in 1907, Oklahoma was designated as "Indian Territory." Former slaves moved to the territory, some even dreaming of the creation of a Black state. They were as bitterly disappointed as those who, half a century earlier, had moved to the "free state" of California. Upon achieving statehood, Oklahoma moved quickly to entrench segregation legislation, severely limiting the political and civil rights of Blacks and igniting a wave of racial violence.

For a few years, Blacks who had moved to Oklahoma set up a separate community in Tulsa, which became a successful economic centre with its own currency, independent businesses, professionals and an infrastructure that included a bus system and an airport. But following a series of riots and Ku Klux Klan attacks that took place over more than a decade, on May 31, 1921, the successful Black Greenwood district, known as the Black Wall Street, was completely destroyed by one of the worst race riots in American history. The district was attacked on the ground and from the air by private planes throwing kerosene bombs, igniting a firestorm that one report says resulted in the death of 3000 people.

Naively, Blacks trying to escape racism in Oklahoma thought that Canada's invitation to settle the prairies included them. However, by 1907–08, when the first settlers tried to move north, the reception at the border was far from friendly. Frank Oliver, Canada's minister of the interior from 1905 to 1911, did all he could to discourage Blacks from entering the country.

Discriminatory medical exams were accompanied for a time by a head tax of $50. Both measures, however, failed to keep out Blacks who were healthy and were able to come up with the necessary resources.

Oliver went further. In 1912 he sponsored an Order in Council that stated, "For a period of one year from and after the date hereof the landing in Canada shall be [sic] and the same is prohibited of any immigrants belonging to the Negro race, which race is deemed unsuitable to the climate and requirements of Canada."

The order was never proclaimed. Political realities required that Canada could not afford to offend the United States. Instead, Oliver sent emissaries to Oklahoma to discourage Black immigration, suggesting, among other things, that they would not be able to cope with the harsh climate. Propaganda said the ground was frozen and covered with snow year round. Oliver was not acting in a vacuum. His actions echoed public sentiment, illustrated by a petition raised in Edmonton in 1911. The Edmonton Board of Trade, supported by the Imperial Order of Daughters of the Empire (IODE) sent a petition to Ottawa, dated April 18, that read in part:

> We, the undersigned residents of the City of Edmonton, respectfully urge upon your attention and that of the Government of which you are the head, the serious menace to the future welfare of a large portion of western Canada, by reason of the alarming influx of negro settlers.
>
> This influx commenced about four years ago in a very small way, only four or five families coming in the first season, followed by thirty or forty families the next year. Last year several hundred negroes arrived at Edmonton and settled in surrounding territory. Already this season nearly three hundred have arrived; and the statement is made,

both by these arrivals and by press dispatches, that these are but an advance guard of hosts to follow. We submit that the advent of such negroes as are now here was most unfortunate for the country, and that further arrivals would be disastrous. We cannot admit as any factor the argument that these people may be good farmers or good citizens. It is a matter of common knowledge that it has been proved in the United States that negroes and whites cannot live in proximity without the occurrence of revolting lawlessness, and the development of bitter race hatred. We want settlers that will assimilate with the Canadian people and in the negro we have a settler that will never do that.

Still, they came.

Between 1900 and 1920, roughly three quarters of a million American immigrants moved into the Prairie Provinces. Of those, only between 1000 and 1500 were Blacks, most arriving between 1907 and the mid-1900s and settling in a few small communities in Alberta and Saskatchewan. The largest and best-known rural settlement was at Amber Valley, 24 kilometres east of the town of Athabasca, Alberta, which celebrated its 100th anniversary in 2009. Other Alberta settlements were established at Junkins, near Wildwood, Keystone, now Breton and Campsie, near present-day Barrhead. In Saskatchewan, a group homesteaded near Maidstone. They erected the tiny Shiloh Baptist Church, which has been declared a historical monument and still stands as a testament to a once thriving community.

Black immigrants tended to establish their settlements away from white communities, preferring to avoid confrontation and discrimination. The choice was a mixed blessing. While the communities were able to achieve

Shiloh Church, the first building erected by the Black community in the Sheldon District, north of Maidstone, Saskatchewan, is an official historical monument. The plaque (on the left) is a tribute to Blacks who settled across the Canadian prairies.

a certain autonomy—building their own schools and churches—having to travel to major centres for supplies, especially in winter, was a hardship. Much has been written about the challenges they faced. What follows are stories of how Black immigrants showed Canadians that they could be good citizens—as good as anyone else.

Across the country, wherever Blacks settled, they created warm, supportive communities and developed social institutions, usually built around the church, which provided recreational and financial as well as spiritual support. But there have always been those who rejected the strictures of small, sometimes inward-looking communities and dared to venture into the wider world. One of the most influential Blacks in Saskatchewan between 1896 and 1915 was not part of the immigrant wave from Oklahoma but a member of an Ontario family who had migrated north via the Underground Railway more than a half century earlier.

Alfred Schmitz Shadd, part of the same family that saw Mary Ann Shadd become a pioneering newspaper publisher, became a leader far from the security of the well-established Black community in southern Ontario. Born in Raleigh, Ontario, in 1869, Shadd is a textbook example of how some Blacks have, throughout our country's history, made the deliberate choice to live and work in mainstream society, somehow developing the coping mechanisms to deal with the prejudices encountered.

Alfred Shadd lived a full and highly successful life, respected and fully accepted by the Saskatchewan community he eventually chose as his home. It's impossible to divine what motivated Shadd to leave the safety and comforts of a prominent, well-established family in Toronto. He may have felt restricted by the mainstream prejudices that always result when Black communities became large enough to be noticed, posing a perceived threat. Maybe he found the Black community to be too insular, too self-isolated. Or he simply may have been born with a pioneer spirit that demanded he seek new frontiers. Whatever the reasons, his story parallels those of many men and women who chose to claim their rightful place in mainstream society, destroying stereotypes, demonstrating success and helping to create the Canada we know today.

Shadd began to study medicine at the University of Toronto, but financial issues forced him to give up that pursuit in favour of a teaching degree. In 1896, at the age of 27, he moved to the Kinistino district, then still part of the Northwest Territories, to work as a teacher. He set up his school in the Agricultural Hall, the centre of social, recreational, political and religious activities. He was the first Black man the community had ever seen. When a little girl sat on his knee and, wetting her finger, tried to see if the colour would rub off of his face, he assured her, quite gently according to reports, that it was permanent.

In addition to teaching, Shadd put his medical knowledge to work. When a man from Birch Hills was brought to him with his head split open, Shadd saved his life. The incident motivated Shadd to set up a small medical practice alongside his teaching. With encouragement from Kinistino citizens, Shadd returned to Ontario to complete his medical degree, graduating with honours from Trinity College at the University of Toronto in 1898. With his new credentials, he returned to Kinistino and set up a full-time medical practice in an office consisting of two rooms, one of which served as his bedroom. Lore has it that he called his operating room "the chamber of horrors" and his bedroom "the chamber of silence."

But it wasn't until Dr. Alfred Shadd moved down the rural road in 1904 to Melfort, a much larger centre, that he created the reputation that led to him being described as "Saskatchewan's great pioneer Black doctor."

He threw himself into community life, opening a drug store, establishing a busy medical practice and becoming a successful farmer. He served on both town council and the school board and was a member of the Board of Trade, the Masonic Order, the Independent Order of Foresters and the Loyal Orange Lodge. He was a founding member and first president of the Melfort Agricultural Society. He also joined the congregation of the All Saints Anglican Church, where he married Jeanette Simpson in 1907. Like many Blacks, then and now, who choose to live and work in mainstream society, he married a white woman. The mixed-race couple had two children, Garrison and Lavina.

Shadd was politically active as a lifelong Conservative. As a member of the municipal council, he supported the creation of the province of Saskatchewan in 1905. He ran for office as a Conservative candidate in Saskatchewan's first election in 1906, losing by only 52 votes. Deciding to promote his political ideas by other means, in 1908 he purchased the *Prince Albert Advocate*, moved it to Melfort and renamed it the *Carrot River Journal*. His Central Drug Store became a profitable enterprise, and its sale funded his entry into publishing. As an award-winning editor, he published articles calling for western rights and fair freight rates and grain prices.

"Plus ça change!" As they say, the more things change, the more they remain the same.

As a farmer, Shadd developed breeding programs for cattle and hogs and raised his own feed. But it was as a physician that he made his mark on the community and earned its respect. A big man with a big laugh, he often put the needs of his patients above his own, making house calls throughout the district, one night delivering both a baby boy and a calf at the same farm. His red 1906 Reo might have been the first car in the district—it was certainly the most well known as he travelled to house calls day and night. Dr. Shadd had his own medical problems, a severe rheumatism that sometimes confined him to bed. But he made light of it, telling people that the Doc never gets sick.

In a major achievement, he led the drive to establish a hospital in Melfort. The Lady Minto Hospital, with support from people throughout the Carrot River Valley, was built in 1906.

Tragically, Shadd's life was too short. In 1915, at the age of 45, he was stricken with acute appendicitis, a very serious illness back then. He was rushed to a hospital in

Winnipeg, but it was too late. He died on March 9, shortly after the operation.

In Melfort, the All Saints Church could not accommodate all of the mourners who gathered for his funeral, which was recorded as the largest ever held in the district. The procession to the cemetery was reported to be a mile long. In his honour his fellow citizens paid to erect a memorial stone at the Mount Pleasant Cemetery.

In his obituary, the *Melfort Moon* states: "No drive was too long; no night too dark; no trail too rough to deter the doctor when the call for assistance came." The naming of Shadd Drive is a testament to the influence and contributions of this remarkable man.

Across the prairies, the new Canadians met their challenges by developing strong community and sports organizations. Jefferson Davis Edwards, his wife, Martha, and their 10 children were among the first families to settle in Pine Creek, near Athabasca, Alberta, which they renamed Amber Valley. In 1926, Edwards established the Amber Valley baseball team. The team played professionally throughout the prairies and was rated one of the best teams in Alberta from the 1920s through to the beginning of World War II, when many players left to join Canada's armed forces.

The baseball team assumed near legendary status, serving as ambassadors not only for Amber Valley but also for all of the Black communities in the province. The athleticism and skill of the team drew large crowds. They were so popular through the years of the Great Depression that they were often guaranteed a $50 appearance fee, win or lose. They played against white baseball teams throughout the province, wearing white uniforms with

From their homebase town near Athabasca, the Amber Valley baseball team played exhibition games throughout Alberta, exhibiting skills almost comparable to those of the famed Harlem Globetrotters basketball team.

"Amber Valley" on the front. On July 1 of each year, they played a match at Lac La Biche in celebration of Canada Day. Much to the delight of the crowd, members of the team were upbeat, joking and talking up the game, their infectious humour gaining them acceptance and support. At a tournament in Grande Prairie, the team won a prize of $300, a considerable sum during the Dirty Thirties.

The Alberta Heritage Foundation's website, a valuable resource for information about all things Alberta, records an "Ode to the Amber Valley Baseball Team," written by Clinton Murphy during the team's heyday in the 1930s:

> We saw "Kenny" in the catcher's slot
> In the days of old renown
> And "Forty" with that side-arm curve

Was hurlin' 'em on the mound
"TC" was out in centre field
So proud he would almost burst
"Man" was playing second
And "Big J" was huggin' first
"Doc" was in at shortstop
No matter what the count might be
You would always hear him yell "tut, tut"
I'll tell the world—it looked pretty good to me
"Alvin Brown" was deep in left
"Moose" was covering right
And down along that third baseline
You were sure to find "Peepsight"
These boys played well together
Known far and wide for their fame
Win, lose or draw, to them
Fairness was the game
They taught us a lesson
You're playing for the team's sake
Play up and the play the game

In individual sports, Amber Valley athletes competed in many provincial and national events. Clinton Murphy was a highly successful boxer who, along with Doug Harper, won provincial and national championships. Whether on the track, on the ice or in the gym, Black athletes did well. These and other activities they excelled in slowly dispelled the fears of the white population, and Blacks gradually became accepted as neighbours, participating in the political, social and economic life of the province.

Among the most notable athletes to come out of the west was Jesse Jones, born in Texas in 1899. He moved to Edmonton with his parents in 1910 and excelled in school, in both academics and in sports. At Victoria High

School he set many track and field records, specializing in the 100-yard sprint, and he was captain of the Victoria Redmen baseball team.

For five years, beginning in 1922, he taught school in the Black community at Keystone, building a basketball court for his students while still competing in track and field. He won 56 amateur track championships and was an inductee of the Alberta Sports Hall of Fame, placing first in the 100-, 220- and 440-yard sprints at the 1923 Olympic trials. But he was unable to attend the Summer Games in Paris. There was little or no government support for Canadian athletes in those days, and he was simply unable to raise the funds to make the trip to Paris. Four years later, Vancouverite Percy Williams, friend and mentor to future Canadian Olympian, Harry Jerome, did receive government support to travel to Amsterdam for the 1928 Olympic Games, and he won the gold medal in the 100- and 200-metre sprints.

Mr. Justice Lionel Jones (centre) with the author (right). Jones was the first Black male lawyer in Alberta.

Jesse Jones' son, Lionel Locksley Jones, who inherited his father's athleticism, was a promising hockey player who might have become the Jarome Iginla of his day. Sadly, an ankle injury ended his hopes of playing professional hockey. Interestingly, he was the best man when runner Harry Jerome married Edmontonian Wendy Foster.

Lionel entered post-secondary education at the University of Alberta in the Department of Physical Education, but he changed his mind and switched to the Faculty of Arts where he earned his first degree. He then enrolled in the School of Law and, after graduation, in 1963, became the first Black male lawyer admitted to the bar in Alberta. He worked as a Crown Prosecutor for the Government of Alberta before being appointed a judge in the Provincial Court. He was subsequently appointed to the Court of Queen's Bench, the first Black to hold the post in Alberta.

Among other academic successes within the Black community of Keystone, Violet King, born to John and Stella King, stands out as the first Black person to graduate from the University of Alberta Law School. In 1954, the year of her graduation, she was called to the bar in Calgary and became the first Black female lawyer in Alberta. She practiced law in Calgary before moving to Ottawa to work with the citizenship branch of the federal government.

Although the populations of other Black communities in Alberta dwindled throughout the 1930s, with many residents moving to larger cities, Amber Valley remained viable into the 1940s with its residents numbering some 350. Many of the descendants of those pioneer families have achieved distinction in careers in Edmonton and Calgary. In recent years a few families have moved

Violet King was the first Black female lawyer to be admitted to the bar in Alberta.

back to farm in the community, which celebrates its existence with an annual picnic.

When Mattie and Joe Mayes and their 10 sons and three daughters arrived in the Eldon district, about 28 kilometres north of Maidstone, Saskatchewan, in March 1910, little did they know that their descendants would make their name famous in the 21st century. They had come a long way—across Oklahoma by wagon train to Tulsa, by train to Winnipeg and North Battleford and then overland to join the tiny community. The Mayes were part of a larger group of immigrants from Oklahoma looking for a new life on the Canadian prairies. Ten or eleven families opted to settle in Eldon, dramatically expanding a Black population that had begun with the arrival of Samuel Boyd in 1907. Others moved on to found the community of Amber Valley.

For $10, the new settlers could take possession of a quarter section of land (160 acres), with the proviso that they had to "prove" the homestead within three years by clearing at least 40 acres of the land, by building a house and by planting crops. If you fly across western Canada on a clear day, you can see the way the land was divided up into sections, each one-mile square, or 640 acres. Early homesteaders built their homes on the "home quarter" adjacent to a neighbour, so that you often see a pattern of four houses, with barns and other outbuildings, clustered together at the corners of their sections. Many thousands of people who came to Canada during that period thought it was the best deal in North America. By the 1920s, 50 families had settled in the community, enough to support the diminutive Shiloh Baptist Church, erected in 1912, with Joe Mayes as the first preacher. A school was opened in 1915.

One of the highlights of the television series *Hymn to Freedom* was a visit to the Shiloh Baptist Church in Eldon with Eleanor Collins. Shiloh Church was designated as an historical site in 1991 and has been lovingly preserved. In the tiny building, which could easily fit into the backyard of many a contemporary urban home, I listened as Ms. Collins sang *a cappella*, reprising an old hymn with such feeling that it sent shivers down the spines of both myself and the film crew.

Eleanor Collins is one of the most luminous descendants of the families who, early in the 20th century, came up from Oklahoma to settle in the Canadian west. Her family arrived in Edmonton, after an arduous trip from Oklahoma, in 1906. The family had to walk 106 miles (170 kilometres) from Edmonton to their homestead at Junkins, the first Black community in Alberta near the present-day Wildwood. Eleanor's mother, Estella May

Eleanor Collins, 75, appearing in the 1994 documentary, *Hymn to Freedom*

Cowan, wrote in her journal, "It was so cold that the children nearly strangled getting their breath."

The land was rough and swampy, but there were lots of berries, fish and wild game, and the settlers planted gardens to provide them with fresh vegetables. Life was hard, but no one starved.

As Eleanor Collins said years later, "Freedom was worth anything that was going to be required of them." As was almost always the case, the first building the community erected was a church.

Eleanor (born "Elnora Ruth") came into the world in Edmonton in 1919. Still in elegant good health, she celebrated her 90th birthday in Vancouver on November 21, 2009.

Eleanor was 15 when she won her first amateur singing contest, and in a heartbeat, she was singing on broadcasting pioneer Dick Rice's Edmonton radio station CFRN. Eleanor made her television debut on CBC

Eleanor Collins. *The Eleanor Show* was the first musical program to be hosted by a woman of any colour on the CBC national television network.

Vancouver in 1954 on a show called *Bamboula*. The next year, *The Eleanor Show* was launched on the CBC television network. She was the first woman, of any colour, to host her own national television show. "I didn't see a lot of my people on TV," she reflected. "I didn't have an example in the beginning because that was not the thing yet."

Other shows followed, including another television variety series simply called *Eleanor,* in 1964. You can find clips of her performances on the CBC Internet site, including a program with Tommy (Senator) Banks' big band, broadcast in 1980.

Perhaps the most famous descendant of Maidstone, Saskatchewan, the community that came to be known as "the Shiloh people," is Rueben Mayes, great grandson of Mattie and Joe, who became a North American football star. Rueben was born on June 6, 1963, in North Battleford, Saskatchewan, where the families of many of the people who had homesteaded in Eldon moved during and after World War II. He played in the U.S. National Football League from 1986 to 1993, setting single game (357 yards), single-season (1632 yards) and career (3519 yards) rushing records. During his NFL career, he carried the ball 866 times for 3484 yards.

Another great grandson of the Mayes family who has achieved 21st-century prominence is Malcolm Mayes, the award-winning editorial cartoonist for the *Edmonton Journal*. His cartoons, funny, biting and insightful, have been published in hundreds of publications, including *Reader's Digest* and scores of major newspapers in Canada and the United States. When the Mayes family held a reunion in 2008, some 300 people attended.

JOHN WARE

One of the best-known Blacks to have come to Alberta during its pioneer days was John Ware (1845–1905). With schools and awards named for him, and biographies written by former Alberta Lieutenant-Governor Grant MacEwan and by Ian Hundey, Ware has risen to near folk-hero status.

Ware was born near Georgetown in South Carolina, and his early years were spent in slavery. Like many of his era who sought a better life in Canada, Ware started life as another man's property. He picked cotton on a plantation. After gaining freedom following the American Civil War (1861–65), Ware, a big strong 19-year-old, went west to Texas where his extraordinary strength and his talent with livestock earned him a reputation as an outstanding cowboy. It seemed he was born to be in the saddle.

In 1882 he joined a drive that drove 3000 cattle from Montana to the North West Cattle Company Ranch, also known as the Bar U—the brand that ranchers burned into the hides of cattle to identify their property—near Calgary. The drive lasted from May to September, and Ware immediately took a liking to the area that was still the North-West Territories of Canada. He worked at the Bar U for a few years and was then persuaded to move to a job at the Quorn Ranch near Sheep Creek. The Quorn was the property of a British hunt club located in Leicestershire, England, and its main purpose was to raise horses for export to the British market. John Ware's growing reputation as a horseman elevated him to a role that put him in charge of the ranch's equine livestock.

The *MacLeod Gazette* said, "John is not only one of the best natured and most obliging fellows in the country, but he is one of the shrewdest cow men, and the man is considered pretty lucky who has him to look after his interest. The horse is not running on the prairie which John cannot ride." The RCMP hired him to break their horses.

It was Ware's near legendary strength that impressed the ranching community. He was a pioneer member of the Calgary Stampede, where his demonstrated ability to wrestle steers became a popular highlight of the event that continues as a major competition to this day. It was said that he could stop a steer head-on, throw it to the ground and quickly tie the beast's feet together. Some reports said that he could lift an 18-month-old steer and flip it on its back. Ware won the first steer-wrestling competition at the Calgary Stampede in 1893. Even though people around the Stampede treated him as a kind of mascot and nicknamed him "Nigger John," Ware rose above the stereotype to become a real contributor to the building of the province as an expert who shared his knowledge in the raising of cattle and horses.

It wasn't long before John Ware had registered his own cattle brand, 9999. It's likely that he took part of his wages in the form of livestock. Later, in 1898, he reregistered the brand as 999. And he became a family man. In 1892 he married the daughter of a Black homesteader who had moved to Calgary from Toronto. Daniel V. Lewis had moved north from his birthplace in Virginia and, after some time in Ontario, decided life would be better in the west. And he had a daughter! John soon acquired a wagon and went a'courting. There's a story that says that while he was taking his future in-law's family out for a ride, a storm blew up and lightning struck the horses, killing both animals instantly. Ware moved the horses out of their traces, took their place and led the family safely home.

Mildred Lewis and John Ware were married in Calgary's First Baptist Church. The *Calgary Tribune,* in noting the event, reported: "probably no man in the district has a greater number of warm personal friends than the groom."

By the late 1890s, the battle between ranchers and settlers—the subject of many a Hollywood cowboy saga—in the area south of Calgary was being lost. Ranchers were pushed eastward onto the less populated prairie. John Ware owned a small property near the foothills and spent $1000 to buy a property on the Red Deer River near the present town of Rosebud, where he moved his herd of some 200 cattle. It was a good place for his growing family; he and Mildred already had two daughters and two sons. In a heartrending harbinger of things to come, the Red Deer River flooded, destroying their first home. They quickly rebuilt, and things seemed to have

John Ware, Alberta's legendary Black cowboy, with his wife Mildred and two of their children. Ware was the creator of the cow-roping attraction at the Calgary Stampede.

righted themselves. The ranch prospered with the herd growing to 1000 head.

Sadly, the family's dream of a long, happy life on the Red Deer River ranch was not to be. Two sons born on the new homestead died in infancy, not an uncommon occurrence in pioneer days. A greater calamity struck three years after they had settled into their new home; Mildred contracted typhoid fever and pneumonia and died. The final blow was an ironic tragedy. The man who could handle any horse met his demise when his horse caught one of its hooves in a badger hole and fell, landing squarely on the rider. John Ware was riding with his son, Bob, who reported that he died instantly. The funeral, held in Calgary on September 14, was said to be the largest to that date and attracted ranchers and horsemen from all over southern Alberta. Ware had become a local hero. The last of his children to survive, Nettie, passed away in 1998 at the age of 96.

John Ware is recognized today at Ware Creek, John Ware Ridge and Mount Ware, near the site of his first ranch. There is also the John Ware High School in southwest Calgary, the John Ware Building at the Southern Alberta Institute of Technology School, and the John Ware 4-H Beef Club in Duchess, Alberta. In 1958 the log cabin that was his home was moved to become part of Dinosaur Provincial Park on the Red Deer River. The cabin, restored and rededicated in 2002, has become a popular tourist site.

It's not that John Ware, a legend in his own time, did not face prejudice and discrimination. He was denied access to certain public services and was harassed by police who, on one occasion, arrested him for no good reason. Some suggest that the nickname "Nigger John" by which he was known to his friends, was, in the context of the times, used as an expression of affection rather than derision. And, with few other Blacks in the community, the affection, even if bordering on condescension, was probably, for the most part, genuine. The true measure of the man was that he was able to rise above such indignities to show the world that he was as good as anybody else, and a lot better than many. Historians remember him as having possessed a good sense of humour and a rock-solid religious faith.

CHAPTER FIVE

STRENGTH FROM STRENGTH: THE BLACK CHURCH

The story of how the Blacks created Canada cannot be told without understanding the central role of the church. Many of the women and men whose stories are told in this book derived their strength, their philosophical underpinnings and their will to confront adversity from profound faith in the basic tenets of Christianity. From James Douglas to Josiah Henson to William Pearly Oliver to Eleanor Collins, the church nourished Black trailblazers. To this day, Black churches across Canada, with the strength and optimism found in rousing gospel music and fiery, colloquial sermons often misunderstood by mainstream observers, produce and sustain trailblazers and game changers. We see it in the sometimes over-the-top demonstrations of athletes thanking their Lord out loud for a touchdown or an ace, in the exuberance of jazz and in the quiet dignity of sleeping car porters who endured unthinking denigration by their customers and advised them as Stanley Grizzle did, that "My Name's Not George."

Members of mainstream society find it difficult to understand the obstacles, both external and internal, that impede the ability of minorities to succeed. Too often they have to work twice as hard for less remuneration than their fellow white citizens.

This is not to say that all Blacks are religious. Many are not. But even in the 21st century, when churches everywhere in the developed world are losing ground, the Black church is holding fast. So when they succeed in the larger world, many adherents credit the principles they learned in church as their inspiration and their bulwark.

Across the Prairies, in southern Ontario and in Nova Scotia—home of what was, until the latter part of the 20th century, the largest Black community in Canada—people were able to endure the hardships they faced because of their deep Christian faith. Because Blacks were either unwelcome or received paternalistic and sometimes degrading treatment in white congregations, they found solace within the protective embrace of their own churches.

One of the best examples of how the church helped to sustain life in Black communities is contained within the story of the Reverend William Pearly Oliver, an early member of an illustrious Nova Scotia family. The family includes world famous singer, Portia White; Donald Havelock Oliver, current member of the Canadian Senate; actor Anthony Sherwood *(Street Legal);* and award-winning contemporary poet and playwright George Elliott Clarke.

Both William Oliver's father and grandfather worked at Acadia University. His grandfather, William II (1850–1934), was essentially a janitor whose responsibility among other things was to stoke the stoves in the university's classrooms. He served the university for more than 40 years and was recognized later in life with the honorary designation of Superintendent of Buildings and Grounds. His son, Clifford (1884–1966), worked with his father and served Acadia in the same role, for 60 years. Father and son were recognized and respected—even if somewhat patronizingly—in the university community.

The Oliver family lived a relatively comfortable life in mainstream society in Wolfville, where William Pearly Oliver was born in 1912. "Billy," as he was called as a boy, was the only Black kid in the neighbourhood, but he had a more secure life than Blacks who lived in the de-facto segregated communities around Halifax. He faced relatively little prejudice as he excelled academically and in sports. His story reflects the frequent but universal reality that when a single Black family establishes itself in a white community, it is rarely seen as a threat, and its members are allowed to participate in activities with relatively few barriers.

But there were incidents. On one occasion, a white hockey team refused to take to the ice if Billy was allowed to play. His teammates, to their credit, refused to play without him, and the game was cancelled. Excelling in sports, Billy was captain of both the football and hockey teams in his senior year.

After graduating from high school with excellent marks, William enrolled in the pre-med program at Acadia University, but he soon decided that his real interest was in the ministry. He graduated with a Bachelor of Arts in 1934 and, two years later, completed his Bachelor of Divinity.

The White and Oliver families were united with the second marriage of William Pearly's father, Clifford.

He was first married to Dorothea Moore in 1910, but they separated in 1921. His second marriage was to Helena White, one of Reverend White's daughters, and a sister to the world famous opera singer Portia White. But it was the White side of the family that set the first example of how Blacks could make their mark in Nova Scotia.

Reverend William Andrew White (1874–1936) was the second Black man to graduate from Acadia University. He earned a degree in theology in 1903 and was later honoured with a Doctorate of Divinity. Following graduation he served as a travelling missionary for the African Baptist Churches of Nova Scotia. Founded in 1832 by Richard Preston, a former slave who came to Canada in 1815, the Baptist church has a long and continuing tradition of serving the province's Black community. In 1854, Preston also founded the African Union Baptist Association (AUBA) that included 12 congregations anchored by the Cornwallis Church. The AUBA later became a strong political force in support of the Nova Scotia Black community.

In 1916, Reverend White enlisted with the No. 2 Construction Battalion (also known as The Black Battalion) during World War I as a commissioned officer with the rank of captain. He was the first Black chaplain to serve with the British armed forces. After the war he served at the Cornwallis Street Baptist Church in Halifax for 17 years, preceding William Pearly Oliver who was called to the church in 1937.

Portia White was not the only member of Reverend White's family to make significant contributions to Canada and Nova Scotia. His son, Bill Jr., ran for Parliament as a candidate for the Co-operative Commonwealth Federation (CCF) in the 1949 federal election. Another son, Jack, became a noted labour union activist and ran for office in the Ontario legislature. Jack's grandchildren include Senator Don Oliver, political strategist Sheila White and folk singer Chris White. George Elliott Clarke, the poet, novelist and playwright, is Jack's great grandson.

Some family.

More about them later.

William Pearly Oliver started his career in the church but left to work in adult education and was a lifelong activist in the fight against discrimination against Blacks. He believed passionately that the church had a vital role in sustaining the Black population. "Its history is in reality the history of our people," he said. "Psychological needs were satisfied through a faith that enabled them to escape from reality. The churches provided indigenous leadership in Black communities."

Oliver's wife, A. Pearleen (Borden) was no less prominent in Nova Scotia's Black community. She was the first Black graduate of the New Glasgow High School and was known as an inspiring public speaker. She served in roles ranging from choir director to author and historian and was in the forefront of the struggle for human rights. In 1976 she was elected as Moderator of the African United Baptist Association of Nova Scotia, the first woman to hold this position. Dr. Pearleen Oliver was recognized with honorary doctorates from Mount St. Vincent and St. Mary's universities.

In the later years of his ministry, William Pearly Oliver became more militant. In a 1968 speech, he said:

> [White] Christians may be quite fundamental about the reality of God and insist upon the literal interpretation of His word, but refuse to acknowledge the brotherhood

of man. The white Christian says to the Black Christian: YOU MAY BE MY BROTHER IN CHRIST, BUT YOU WILL CERTAINLY NEVER BE MY BROTHER-IN-LAW.

Feeling the need for action beyond the pulpit, Oliver founded the Nova Scotia Association for the Advancement of Coloured People (NSAACP) in 1945, an organization geared to improving the standard of living conditions for Blacks in Nova Scotia. By 1962, Oliver felt he had to move on from his role in the church. After some years as a part-time consultant, he became a full-time employee of the Nova Scotia Adult Education Branch. Education, he believed, was the real key to success for Black youth. "To educate a Negro is to unfit him for a servant," he said.

A continuing presence in the leadership of Nova Scotia's Black community, Oliver was present when the sod was turned on April 24, 1982, for the construction of the Black Cultural Centre. The first board of directors included Senator Don Oliver, Carrie Best and H.A.J. (Gus) Wedderburn (brother of the late human rights activist Rosemary Brown). The centre, an attractive building located at 1149 Main Street in Halifax, includes a museum and archives, an auditorium and The Rev. Dr. W.P. Oliver Hall of Fame, named in his honour.

William Pearly Oliver died peacefully at home in May 1989.

Across Canada, the church continues to play a central role in the lives of Black communities. A good example can be found in Montreal, where the Union United Church met the spiritual needs of railway porters who worked on the CPR as well as the community that grew up around Windsor Station. The still vibrantly active church was founded in 1907 after Blacks were refused admission to white churches. It is the home of Montreal's oldest Black congregation. Canadian icons such as musician Oscar Peterson, actor Percy Rodrigues, novelist Mairuth Sarsfield and the Honourable Judge Juanita Westmoreland-Traoré were members of the church, which continues to offer numerous educational and recreational programs for families.

The Coloured Women's Club of Montreal, beginning as a social club in 1900, played a central role in the creation of the Union Church. Its members raised money for everything from furniture, carpeting and linen to the church's christening font. They provided books and bursaries for Black students, and the club was a critical social service agency rendering assistance to members of the community wherever it was needed. During the great flu pandemic of World War I, the club maintained

Montreal's Union United Church has been the bedrock of a strong Black community from its founding in 1907 to the present day. The women of the church offered support to the less fortunate during the Depression years.

facilities at the Grace Dart Hospital. Its members visited patients and helped look after their homes and children. Through the years of the Great Depression, the club operated soup kitchens and served as nurses and mothers' aides. The women also purchased a plot in the Mount Royal Cemetery in which members of the Black community could be buried.

Annual picnics were among the highlights of the social season. But it was the church services that really cemented the community. Members of the congregation dressed in their finest Sunday outfits, and one of the more entertaining Sunday morning features were the hats worn by the women of the church. As a child, I was fascinated by the display of millinery, often elaborate and homemade. To this day, if you attend a Black church anywhere in Canada, the women wear hats. The informal gatherings after the church service also provided an important venue for sharing ideas, concerns and fellowship.

Members of the church remember the leadership of the Reverend Charles H. Este (1896–1977) who took up the pulpit in 1923 while he was in the last year of his degree in theology. His pioneering efforts were instrumental in a cross-Canada effort to unite Black congregations affiliated with the Presbyterian, Methodist and Congregational churches. In 1925 Este officially assumed the role of full-time minister of the newly amalgamated Union United Church. He served in this position until his retirement in 1968.

The experience of the Montreal church is replicated, with local variations, in almost every Black community in Canada. Many are famous for their gospel choirs and for their often rollicking, fervently enthusiastic services led by preachers who move their congregations to laughter and to tears, and when needed, to action. If you ask Blacks to reflect on the essential element binding their communities, many would describe themselves as a spiritual people. The tight embrace of Christianity reflects a yearning for the dignity, fairness and justice embodied by Jesus Christ—for an inclusive brotherhood in which all men and women are equal. Without the sustenance they derived from the church, it's unlikely that many of the Blacks who helped to create Canada could have succeeded.

CHAPTER SIX

THE NOVA SCOTIANS: A REMARKABLE COMMUNITY

Nova Scotia was home to one of the earliest and, up to the recent past, the largest Black population in Canada. Perhaps because their numbers caused them to be perceived as a threat to the white community, Black Nova Scotians suffered more severe discrimination than other communities spread across the country. Blacks came to Nova Scotia with the Empire Loyalists and were technically entitled to the same privileges and land grants available to white Loyalists. But it was not to be. Those Blacks who did get access to land were given the least productive plots in the least attractive locations. The bulldozing of the Halifax ocean-side community of Africville in the late 1960s remains an open sore on the history of race relations in that province.

And yet, in the face of adversity, the Black community of Nova Scotia has produced, and continues to produce, remarkable individuals who contribute to the ongoing

A small monument in an empty field is a reminder of the poor but strong community of Africville, birthplace of many Black Canadians who later helped to change Canada.

creation of Canada. We've already seen the contribution of the White-Oliver families to the building of their church. And other members of this extraordinary family have made their mark.

PORTIA WHITE

Portia White was one of the brightest stars to emerge from Nova Scotia's Black community. A member of an illustrious family that continues to contribute to the creation of Canada in significant ways, she was the aunt to both Senator Donald Oliver and George Elliott Clarke. Portia carved her own place in the firmament with a stunningly beautiful voice. Through training and discipline, she shaped her vocal talent into an instrument that took her around the world.

Portia was born June 24, 1911, in Truro, the third of 13 children born to Reverend William Andrew White and Izie Dora White. Portia's brother, Bill, was the first Canadian of African heritage to run for political office in Canada, standing as a candidate for the CCF, forerunner of today's New Democratic Party, in 1949. Bill's children included politician Sheila White, and Chris White, a folk musician. Another brother, Jack, became a well-known union leader. And Portia's youngest brother, Lorne, sang on the *Singalong Jubilee* TV program that featured Anne Murray.

Like all children in her community, Portia attended church regularly and sang in the choir, first at the Zion Baptist Church in Truro at the age of six, then later at the Cornwallis Street Baptist Church in Halifax when her father assumed the ministry. An older sister, Helena, was the organist. Reverend White organized concerts featuring the choir to raise money for the church. Portia was still a teenager when she became choir director.

It was clear that her rich mezzo-soprano voice was exceptional. Encouraged by her parents, she took voice lessons, walking 16 kilometres into Halifax once a week. But she also prepared herself for the practical world, enrolling in a teacher training program and earning $30 per month teaching at Lucasville, one of the many Black settlements around Halifax. She won the Helen Kennedy Silver Cup at the Nova Scotia Music Festival in 1935, 1937 and 1938. Her success encouraged the Halifax Ladies Music Club to fund a scholarship that allowed her to study at the Halifax Conservatory of Music with Dr. Ernesto Vinci, who helped Portia to develop her voice into a rich contralto.

Portia performed in her first recital in Halifax in June 1939, continuing with performances at Acadia and Mount Allison universities in 1940. During the war years, she appeared frequently on radio and, with members of her family as the "White Quartette," entertained troops in the port-of-debarkation city. One of her strongest mainstream supporters was Dr. Edith Read, a native of Halifax who was the principal of Branksome Hall, an exclusive school for girls in Toronto. Read arranged for Portia's national Canadian debut in a recital at the Eaton Auditorium in Toronto in 1941. The contemporary critic Hector Charlesworth noted in the *Globe and Mail*: "she sings Negro spirituals with pungent expression and beauty of utterance." The *Toronto Telegram*'s Ed Wodson described her voice as a "coloured and beautifully shaded contralto all the way....It is a natural voice, a gift from heaven."

Portia was 31 when she stepped onto the international stage in March 1944. It was Edith Read who had arranged for an audition for Portia with Edward Johnson, a Canadian who was the manager of the Metropolitan Opera. The concert, at the famous Town Hall in New York City, featured songs and arias from the classical repertoire, as well as a selection of so-called Negro spirituals. She played to a packed house and drew rave reviews. Critics noted her remarkable voice and musicianship, her diction and her gracious stage presence. After a second Town Hall performance in October, a newspaper headline declared, "An Unheralded Star Is Born."

Portia's career blossomed into a series of world tours, appearing in concerts in the United States, Latin America, Switzerland and France, as well as across Canada. In Panama she was given a gold medal for her "distinguished cultural services and the promotion of human relations." At the creation of the United Nations in 1948, she performed in the United Nations Festival.

In 1952 she settled in Toronto and taught music to students at Edith Read's Branksome Hall. In 1964, in one of her last major public appearances, Portia performed for Queen Elizabeth II at the opening of the renowned Prince Edward Island Confederation Centre of the Arts in Charlottetown. She described the event as the crowning achievement of her career.

Portia White yielded to cancer on February 13, 1976; she was only 57. She has been recognized as "a person of national historic significance" by the Government of Canada and is featured in the millennium postage stamp series celebrating Canadian achievement.

DONALD HAVELOCK OLIVER

One of the members of the Oliver-White family who is helping to create Canada in the 21st century is Portia White's nephew, Don Oliver, a devoted human rights activist and a member of the Canadian Senate. Oliver was raised in a family that placed a great deal of importance on education and community service. And he decided early in life that becoming a lawyer would satisfy both imperatives. The family history would expect no less.

Born in Wolfville on November 16, 1938, Oliver earned a BA (Honours) in history at Acadian University and an LLB degree from the storied faculty of law at Dalhousie University. He soon earned the designation of Queen's Counsel and maintained a close connection with Dalhousie, teaching lawyers as a part-time professor while running a full-time law practice from 1965 until 1990. On September 7, 1990, he was appointed to the Canadian Senate by Prime Minister Brian Mulroney. A lifelong Conservative, Oliver was active in party affairs, serving at various times as the party's

Senator Don Oliver is a champion of Black causes in his home province of Nova Scotia, in the Senate and across Canada. He was part of the delegation when Prime Minister Harper went to Washington to meet President Obama in October 2009.

head of legal affairs as well as a vice president of the federal party.

Along the way Don Oliver became a successful business-man and farmer, raising Christmas trees for export. But it is for his commitment to human rights in general and issues facing the Black community in particular that Blacks across Canada will remember him. He, along with his half-brother William Pearly Oliver, was one of the supporters of Halifax's Black Cultural Centre,

an important community centre, museum and reposi-
tory of the history of Blacks in Nova Scotia. Both men
were involved in the creation of the Nova Scotia
Association for the Advancement of Coloured Peoples.
Donald was also the founding president of the Society
for the Protection and Preservation of Black Culture in
Nova Scotia. He helped to create the Chair on Canadian
Black Studies at Dalhousie University and is a co-chair
of a campaign to establish the Michaëlle Jean Chair in
Canadian Caribbean and African Diasporic Studies at the
University of Alberta. Among his many other community
initiatives, he is part of a movement to form a business-
based, national Black organization in Canada. As a senator,
he maintains a speaking schedule that sees him lecturing
on both Black and general human rights issues. The following excerpt from one of his speeches might well have
served as an introduction to this book:

> Our intellectual, cultural and indeed spiritual emanci-
> pation will only really begin when we succeed in destroy-
> ing the artificial barriers imposed by stereotypes com-
> monly held about us. Only then will Canadians start to see
> Blacks as we really are; a people of countless success
> stories. A people who have excelled in academia, sports,
> science and religion. A people who by the force of their
> character and their sheer determination to succeed, have
> prospered in an often hostile environment. If we can
> achieve this, if we can dispel the myths and prejudices,
> my hope is the stereotypes will wither and die. We will then
> be in a position to engage in a dialogue of equals.

Senator Donald Oliver has been recognized with
honorary degrees from the universities of Guelph and
Dalhousie as well as receiving the Harry Jerome Award
for Community Service. He is scheduled to retire from

the Senate in 2013, but it is highly unlikely that he will retire from advocacy.

Two other contemporary descendents of the Oliver-White family are making their marks across Canada in the 21st century: George Elliott Clarke and Anthony Sherwood.

GEORGE ELLIOTT CLARKE

George Elliott Clarke, PhD, is an award-winning poet playwright and author of a number of scholarly works. A dynamic lecturer and an animated reader/performer of poetic works, he was the first Black man to win the Governor General's Award for English Poetry, in 2001. He is a tenured professor of English at the University of Toronto. Fittingly, he was the first winner of the $25,000

George Elliott Clarke, winner of the Governor General's Award for English Poetry, is one Canada's most celebrated poets and playwrights.

Portia White Prize presented by the Nova Scotia Arts Council. He has written for the stage and for the screen. His first feature film, *One Heart Broken Into Song* (1999), was directed by Clement Virgo, and his first opera, *Beatrice Chancy* (composed by James Rolfe), starred Measha Brueggergosman, who was, in fact, "discovered" when she sang the lead role.

Born in Windsor, Nova Scotia, in 1960, Clarke is part of the White-Oliver family that has been in Canada for seven generations. His sparkling, dynamic, "with it" personality destroys stereotypes on contact, his brilliance erasing any vestiges of perception that Blacks are somehow different and not as good.

Clarke is an officer of the Order of Canada and a member of the Order of Nova Scotia. He was awarded the $225,000 Trudeau Fellowship, presented to the finest thinkers in the humanities and social sciences. He has won the Rockefeller Foundation Bellagio Centre (Italy) fellowship and the Dartmouth Book Award for fiction. He is also the recipient of six honorary doctorates.

ANTHONY SHERWOOD

Anthony Sherwood has been a member of the Canadian acting fraternity for more than a quarter of a century. Born in Halifax, raised in Montreal, he has been a producer and a director as well as an actor. He has performed in more than 30 feature films and numerous television programs and series, including the award-winning *Street Legal*. He has shared stage and screen with the likes of Henry Fonda, Burt Reynolds, Sidney Poitier and Lou Gossett Jr. But he remains stalwartly Canadian, producing documentaries for the CBC in addition to developing film and television projects.

JAMES ROBINSON JOHNSTON

Senator Oliver was instrumental in the creation of a chair at Dalhousie University honouring a man who preceded him in his profession and who was an early trailblazer for Black professionals in Nova Scotia. James Robinson Johnston was born in Halifax in 1876, the son of William Johnston and the grandson of the Reverend James Thomas. Typically, the church was an important influence in his upbringing. His membership in the Cornwallis Street Baptist Church greatly influenced his development. He was just 10 years old when he joined the African United Baptist Union, becoming superintendent of the Sunday School, and later organizing the Baptist Youth Provincial Union.

Johnston entered university at 16, earned a Bachelor of Letters degree at the age of 20 and graduated with a Bachelor of Law degree in 1898. He was the first Black to graduate from the Dalhousie Law School. He was admitted to the Nova Scotia Bar in 1900 and carried on an active practice in military and criminal law. "Lawyer Johnston" as he was known, believed that education was the key to advancement, and, among other initiatives, he helped to establish an agricultural and industrial school for Black youth.

He was active in community affairs and in politics as a member of the Conservative Party. Historians say that, had his life not been cut tragically short, he might well have been the first Black judge in the province. In his most famous trial, he represented James Murphy, accused of killing a 64-year-old widow with a sledgehammer. The details of the case are fascinating, but the real story is how Johnston used his considerable powers of rhetoric to produce a hung jury at the first trial and an acquittal at the second. The presiding judge, Mr. Justice

James Johnston Ritchie, acknowledged Johnston's brilliance in his summation to the jury at the first trial, which failed to reach a verdict after six hours of deliberation: "This was a decidedly clever, ingenious and well delivered argument and reflects great credit on the counsel...."

On March 2, 1915, James Robinson Johnston was shot to death by his wife's brother, Harry Allen. Reports suggest that there was bad blood between the two men and allegations that Robinson had a violent temper that was sometimes directed at his wife. Allen, found guilty at trial and sentenced to death, had his sentence commuted to life imprisonment. The potentially mitigating circumstances of the murder are reflected by the fact that, in the end, he served only 14 years in prison.

Lawyer Johnston was undoubtedly the most prominent Black man of his era. His death led to a public outcry; some 10,000 people, Black and white, attended his funeral on the Sunday afternoon of March 7. It was said to be the largest funeral in the province since that of Prime Minister Sir John S.D. Thompson 20 years earlier. Johnston's body lay in state at the Cornwallis Street Baptist Church; there were so many flowers that it took three carriages to take them to the graveyard. Prime Minister Robert Borden, in a telegram, decried the loss of what he described as an "ornament" to the practice of law.

But because Johnston was the victim of what we describe today as a "Black on Black" crime, his murder was followed by an overwhelming sense of embarrassment among his own people. Had his killer been white, had this been a racially motivated crime, he would have been celebrated as a hero and a martyr. Instead, many in the mainstream perceived his death as just another illustration of life in the minority community, producing, according to one report:

> ...consternation among whites, and reinforced negative racial stereotypes which distorted even the judicial view of the case. If the Black community could not preserve the life of their own chief of men, a member of the learned professions whom the white establishment accepted as an equal, what indeed was to become of them?

These sentiments may explain why it wasn't until 1991 that the name of James Robinson Johnston was restored to prominence. After a fundraising campaign supported by Senator Donald Oliver and Blacks all across Canada, the Dalhousie Law School established the James Robinson Johnston Chair in Black Canadian Studies.

CALVIN WOODROW RUCK

In the summer and fall of 1993, I was privileged to travel across the country as host of *Hymn to Freedom*, a four-hour television documentary series produced by Almeta Speaks, a remarkable woman who has carved out a multi-faceted career ranging from composer/singer/recording artist to documentary producer to historian to academic. The series borrowed its title, but not its music, from the Oscar Peterson song of the same title. Speaks composed the music for the series, which chronicled the life and challenges of Black individuals and communities in Nova Scotia, Quebec, Ontario and western Canada. My role included interviewing scores of people who are part of the story of Blacks in Canada. The Nova Scotia interviewees included Burnley "Rocky" Jones and Calvin Ruck, a tireless, lifelong advocate and activist in support of Black causes.

On a sunny Saturday morning, on July 10, 1993, I joined several hundred people gathered in Pictou, Nova Scotia, to commemorate the No. 2 Construction Battalion that served in World War I from 1916 to 1920. Known as The Black Battalion, it was described by Calvin Ruck as "Canada's best kept military secret." The welcome but long overdue event was celebrated with much pomp and ceremony. Among the dignitaries gathered for the ceremony were Nova Scotia Lieutenant-Governor Mayann E. Francis, O.N.S.; federal cabinet minister Peter MacKay; Rear Admiral Paul Maddison, Commander, Joint Task Force, Atlantic; Senator Donald Oliver, Q.C.; and Oliver's brother Leslie Oliver, president of the Black Cultural Society of Nova Scotia. Calvin Ruck gave an impassioned keynote address, relating the

The late Calvin Ruck fought to gain recognition for the No. 2 Construction Battalion that served overseas during World War I.

On July 10, 1993, several hundred people gathered in Pictou, Nova Scotia, to commemorate the No. 2 Construction Battalion. Calvin Ruck (in the white hat and black suit) was chiefly responsible for the ceremony honouring the battalion.

efforts he took, over many years, to gain appropriate recognition for the Blacks who fought for Canada during World War I.

A town crier announced the event and called the proceedings to order. There were bagpipes, anthems, handshakes and speeches and, finally, the unveiling of a monument and an interpretive plaque that began with this sentence:

> THE BLACK BATTALION REFLECTED THE STRONG DETERMINATION OF BLACK MEN TO CONTRIBUTE TO CANADA'S FIRST WORLD WAR EFFORT, DESPITE DISCRIMINATION.

The discrimination was virtually cast in concrete. Early attempts of Black men to fight for their country were met with the catchphrase that this was a "white man's war."

They were told that Canada did not want a "checkerboard army" and that white soldiers did not want to serve alongside Blacks. But the people who had struggled to migrate to Canada after generations of slavery in the U.S. were determined to prove their patriotism, to play their part in defending their newfound, if less than perfect, freedom. Black leaders from across the country wrote letters petitioning the federal Minister of Defence Sam Hughes to allow Blacks to serve.

This is one of many letters:

November 6, 1914,
To Sir Sam Hughes Minister of Militia and Defence, Ottawa

Dear Sir:

The colored [sic] people of Canada want to know why they are not allowed to enlist in the Canadian militia. I am informed that several who have applied for enlistment in the Canadian expeditionary forces have been refused for no other apparent reason than their color, as they were physically and mentally fit.

Thanking you in advance for any information that you can & will give me in regards to this matter. I remain yours respectfully, for King & Country.

Arthur Alexander,
North Buxton, Ont.

(Original in Public Archives of Canada, Ottawa)

Hughes responded that if they could find a (white) commanding officer to lead them, he would approve. It took close to two years, but finally Lieutenant Colonel Daniel H. Sutherland agreed to command the unit, and the

Deacon Sidney Morgan Jones (1899–1993), one of the last survivors of the Black Battalion, lived to see its recognition.

first and only Black battalion in Canadian military history was authorized on July 5, 1916. About 1000 men joined the battalion, some 600 of them from Nova Scotia; among them was Deacon Sidney Morgan Jones, grandfather of present-day activist Burnley (Rocky) Jones. I had the privilege of interviewing Deacon Jones while he was living in a nursing home, shortly before his death.

As the name of the battalion implies, the No. 2 was not part of the official fighting forces, and, although some Blacks saw combat action, for the most part, the men carried no weapons. They dug trenches, erected bridges and barricades and defused land mines. They lived in separate quarters from the white soldiers and did the dirty work. The battalion was demobilized from Pictou in 1919 and officially disbanded on September 15, 1920, without any fanfare or recognition. The men (some of whom had enlisted as teenagers) went back to their homes across the country and to a racial environment that had hardly changed since their departure. The veterans faced segregation in housing, employment, education and even in graveyards.

The fact that the battalion was being commemorated so many years later was substantially due to the efforts of Calvin Ruck. He contributed to the creation of Canada by dispelling the myth that World War I was a "white man's war" in which no Black Canadians participated. In one of the two books he published on the subject, Ruck wrote:

> Black Canadians have a long and honourable tradition of patriotism, sacrifice and heroism as loyal citizens serving in the British and Canadian Armed Forces. From the American Revolutionary War (1775–83), Blacks have fought, bled and died on behalf of Empire, King and country.

Born on September 4, 1925, Calvin Ruck was the son of immigrants from Barbados who came to Sidney, Nova Scotia, in the early 1900s. Calvin left school after grade 10 and first worked as a labourer, then as a sleeping car porter on the Canadian National Railway. But seeing no prospect for advancement, he went into business and for some years owned and operated a corner store in Halifax.

From 1968 to 1981, Ruck was employed as a community development worker by the Government of Nova Scotia. During the same period, he went back to school and, in 1979, earned a diploma from the Maritime School of Social Work at Dalhousie University. (The school now awards a Calvin W. Ruck scholarship yearly.)

A tireless crusader for human rights throughout his life, Calvin was a lifelong member of the Nova Scotia Association for the Advancement of Coloured People. He served as a member of the Nova Scotia Human Rights Commission from 1981 to 1986. He organized campaigns against businesses, including barbershops, that refused to serve Blacks, sometimes taking his whole family into a barbershop and refusing to leave until they cut his hair. In 1954 he broke the colour barrier in a white neighbourhood by buying a lot and building a house in the face of petitions against him.

Ruck's efforts were recognized. In 1994, soon after I met him, he was inducted as a member of the Order of Canada. The Order of Canada citation states, "He has been a life-long advocate of social justice, equal opportunities for those who are disadvantaged and respect for people of every race, colour, ethnic background, gender or class. As a social worker and member of many community development organizations in Nova Scotia, he used his gifts for bringing together people with diverse interests in support of various projects."

Both Dalhousie University and the University of King's College awarded him honorary doctorates in 1994. In 1998, Prime Minister Jean Chrétien appointed Ruck to the Senate, where he served until reaching the mandatory retirement age of 75 in 2000.

Calvin Ruck died peacefully at his home on October 19, 2004. He was 79.

WILLIAM EDWARD HALL

It would be highly inappropriate to leave the subject of Black participation in Canada's armed forces without recognizing the bravery of William Hall, a true, and for many years, unsung hero.

In Lucknow, India, in 1857, the HMS *Shannon* was on her way to China when a mutiny against Britain erupted in India. Remember that this is the era when England so dominated the world that it could boast that the sun never set on the British Empire. HMS *Shannon* was ordered to join the battle to relieve Lucknow, where the British garrison was under siege by rebel forces. The *Shannon,* which had been reinforced for battle in Calcutta, sent its gun crews ashore with 24-pound artillery to attack a mosque that had been taken by the rebels. William Hall, a 30-year-old able seaman, was manning one of the cannons and set up a barrage to try to break down the walls of the mosque. But a steady hail of musket and grenade fire from the mosque decimated the *Shannon*'s crew, leaving Hall and the battery's commander, Lieutenant Thomas James Young, as the only survivors. Facing death, Hall and Young kept loading and firing the cannon until the wall of the mosque was breached, allowing British ground forces to turn the tide of the battle.

There are varying accounts of the details of the battle and the causes that led to it, but both men were recommended for the Empire's most prestigious award for bravery, the Victoria Cross. Hall's citation reads:

> William Hall V.C. the first Nova Scotian, and the First Man of colour to win the Empire's highest award for valour. Born at Horton, Nova Scotia, April 28th, 1821. Died at Avonport, Nova Scotia, August 27th, 1904. On November 16th, 1857, when serving in H.M.S. *Shannon*, Hall was part of a crew under command of a Lieutenant which placed a 24-pounder gun near the angle of the Shah Nujjiff at Lucknow, when all

but the Lieutenant and Hall were either killed or wounded. Hall with utter disregard for life kept loading and firing the gun until the wall had been breached and the relief of Lucknow had been assured. His great pride was his British Heritage.

The medal was presented to Hall aboard HMS *Donegal* at Queenstown, Ireland, on October 28, 1859.

William was one of six offspring of Jacob and Lucinda Hall, who had begun their lives as slaves in the American south. Some reports say that they were rescued from slavery by a British frigate during the war of 1812. Perhaps that experience had something to do with the young William's fascination with the sea. As a teenager he worked in the shipyards at nearby Hantsport, helping to build wooden ships for the merchant marine. He was 17 when he "ran away to sea," joining the merchant navy as a seaman. In February 1852, he joined the Royal Navy and was posted aboard the HMS *Rodney,* a ship engaged in fighting the Crimean War. Both the British and the Turks awarded him medals for his participation in the war; he received the Crimean Medal with clasps for Inkerman and Sebastopol, the Turkish Medal and the Indian Medal for the relief of Lucknow.

After the battle at Lucknow, Hall continued his career in the navy, rising to become Quartermaster Petty Officer aboard the HMS *Peterel.* He retired in 1876 and returned without fanfare to live with his sisters on a small family farm in Avonport overlooking the Minas Basin, an inlet of the Bay of Fundy. Recognition of his bravery came with a 1901 visit by the Duke of Cornwall (later King George V). Hall was invited to be part of a parade of veterans, wearing his Victoria Cross and three other service medals. The duke singled him out, inquired about his medals and recognized his accomplishments.

Hall died at home in Avonport on August 27, 1904, and was buried in an unmarked grave without any hint of military honours. It wasn't until 1937 that a movement was launched seeking to have Hall's valour recognized. Eight years later, as World War II was winding down, Hall was reinterred with full honours from the Royal Canadian Legion at the Baptist Church in Hantsport. The site is marked by a substantial stone monument, which has been well maintained by the town of Hantsport. The monument displays an enlarged replica of his Victoria Cross and replicates the citation that accompanied the awarding of the medal. Years later, a branch of the Royal Canadian Legion in Halifax was named in Hall's honour.

In 1967, England returned Hall's medals to Canada where they became part of a display at Expo '67 in Montreal. The medals were later transferred to the Nova Scotia Museum.

BURNLEY A. (ROCKY) JONES

Another Nova Scotian who continues to make a difference is Burnley (Rocky) Jones. Jones now practices street level law in Halifax, offering legal aid to those who cannot afford the regular rates charged by lawyers. But earlier in his life he was part of a movement that brought Black issues, long hidden under the carpet from mainstream Canadians, sharply into the national spotlight. An old black-and-white television news clip from a CBC report sometime in the late '50s shows a young Jones complaining about his inability to rent a place in Toronto. It was one of many experiences in "Toronto the Good" that turned Rocky into a fiercely determined—at the time some would have said radical—fighter for the human rights of Blacks in Canada.

Burnley Jones' father, Elmer, was born in Truro, Nova Scotia, married in 1935 and with his wife, Willena, produced a family of seven girls and three boys. Burnley was the fourth child. Burnley grew up in a warm Black neighbourhood near Truro, part of a family that traces its Canadian roots back to the early 1800s when his great grandfather, Sam Jones, accompanied by his brother, walked up to Canada from the southern U.S. His grandfather, Deacon Sidney Jones, a member of the No. 2 Construction Battalion during World War I, settled in Truro after the war.

Burnley was a restless as a boy, even though he lived in an environment in which it was part of the tradition that everyone looked after everyone else. He tells stories about how older members of the community acted as parents to all of the children, to the extent that they expected other people's kids to run errands for them. And if you got into trouble, your mother would probably know about it before you got home.

"I knew that if I stayed in Truro, that the town would destroy me," he said. "There were no jobs, no future. I had to get out to save myself." At the age of 16 he joined the Royal Canadian Engineers as an apprentice. It was on a troop train to Chilliwack, BC, that he started telling his compatriots, "Don't knock the Rock." The other soldiers replied, "So you think you're rocky," and he's been Rocky ever since. In the late '50s he moved to Toronto, and, among other things, worked as a truck driver. It was early days in the American Civil Rights movement, and people such as Stokely Carmichael (later known as Kwame Toure) were becoming household names. People were demonstrating across the U.S. and Canada, even in Toronto.

Burnley "Rocky" Jones as a young activist during the civil rights movement of the 1960s

Rocky Jones and his first wife, Joan, saw television coverage of a civil rights demonstration in front of the U.S. Consulate on University Avenue.

"All of these white people were demonstrating down at the American consulate—but there were no Black people in the demonstration about Black rights," he said. Rocky and Joan, with a new baby, decided it was important for them to join the demonstration. He was invited to speak, and, almost inevitably, he found himself on national television. That was the moment, in his words, that "this radical was born." Years later, he said, "You don't create history, history creates you." He threw himself into the cause in Toronto and was labelled by some media as the Canadian Stokely Carmichael.

Rocky explains: "I was associated with the Panthers in a very informal way. Stokely Carmichael, the Provisional President, stayed at my house with his wife (the celebrated South African singer) Miriam Makeba. Other members of the Panthers used my house as a safe haven, and I was active in many of their strategy sessions regarding Boston, Roxbury and New York. For intelligence and safety reasons I did not take out a formal membership."

But he and Joan decided that their work was in Nova Scotia, the part of the country in which the largest Black population in the country faced pervasive discrimination. "We formed plans with the Panthers to set up a training facility in Nova Scotia," he said. "We visited the proposed site and this might have happened except that one of the Panthers who was here to help implement the plan was arrested and deported back to the States. This was between 1966 and 1969."

The couple immersed themselves in work as community organizers and persuaded a prominent group of white leaders to support their cause by raising enough money to pay Rocky a modest salary. With no strings attached, he was given *carte blanche* to do what was needed to raise the hopes and the status of Nova Scotia's Black communities. But his plan was not simply to attack the general inequities of the system; he was particularly concerned about the school system, which he said set up Black children for failure. Few went on to high school, and even fewer progressed to post-secondary education.

Rocky helped to create the Hero Oral History Project on Black culture and served as executive director of R.O.P.E. (Real Opportunities for Prisoner Employment). He argued that if kids couldn't get an education, they could not be free. R.O.P.E. was able to raise funds to buy a house on Cunard Street and established the first inner-city self-help programs in Nova Scotia, including a school that was named Kwacha House—"Kwacha" is a Zambian word for "freedom." The school was open to both Black and white children. Although the project had the support of some of Halifax's leading citizens, it was not without adversaries. Late one night, someone splashed coal oil across the back of the building and set it on fire. Several children who were sleeping inside were lucky to escape unscathed.

The Jones family doesn't only talk the talk on the subject of education—they also walk the walk. Rocky's mother, Willena, went back to school in her 50s and, at age 60, graduated from the Nova Scotia Teachers College. Following in her footsteps, Rocky also returned to school later in life, and in 1992 at the age of 50, graduated from Dalhousie Law School. He now practices law in Halifax, taking cases for people who cannot afford fees charged by mainstream lawyers.

"Part of the lesson that all of us were taught when we were growing up is that you are responsible for yourself, and you're responsible for your community. And the more you know, the greater the responsibility," says Rocky.

It took eight years, but one of Rocky Jones' greatest challenges became his greatest triumph. In 1995, three young Black girls, accused of stealing $10, were strip-searched in their school by a white police officer, Constable Carol Campbell. At an ensuing press conference, Jones, and Anne Derrick, a fellow civil rights lawyer who had joined him in representing the girls in a suit against the constable, the school and the City of Halifax, said that the incident had racist undertones and would not have happened if the girls were white and well off.

Constable Campbell, who later adopted her married name of Campbell-Waugh, sued the lawyers for defamation, arguing that they had branded her as a racist. She denied that she had strip-searched the girls but had only

Rocky Jones earned a law degree at the age of 50. His storefront practice in Halifax was dedicated to helping those who could not afford the fees charged by mainstream lawyers, particularly young people.

asked them to pull their panties away from their bodies so that she could look for the 10-dollar bill.

The wheels of justice grind slowly. Six years later, in May 2001, a Supreme Court of Nova Scotia jury found for the plaintiff. The court ordered Jones and Derrick to pay $240,000 in compensatory damages and $105,000 in legal costs. It was one of the highest defamation awards in the history of the province, and it put an immediate chill on civil rights advocacy, not only in Nova Scotia but also across Canada.

Jones and Derrick, of course, appealed to the Nova Scotia Court of Appeal. On October 24, 2002, in a two-to-one decision, the court overturned the original verdict and assessed some $105,000 in legal costs against Constable Campbell-Waugh.

Writing for the majority, Justice Elizabeth Roscoe and Chief Justice Constance Glube, the court said:

If constitutional rights are to have any meaning, they must surely include the freedom of persons whose Charter guarantees have been deliberately violated by officials of state agencies, to cry out loud and long against their transgressors in the public forum, and in the case of children and others less capable of articulation of the issues, to have their advocates cry out on their behalf. [Jones and Derrick] had a duty to speak about the events at the school, the complaints filed against the respondent and the Charter breaches they reasonably understood had taken place.

The lawsuit filed against the police officer by the girls and their parents was settled out of court; the terms of the settlement were not revealed. But that's not the end of the story. The police and the school sought leave to appeal the Court of Appeal's decision to the Supreme Court of Canada. On May 30, 2003, some eight years after the precipitating incident, the *Halifax Herald* reported that the Supreme Court had refused to take the case.

That ended it. Claims have been made on all sides justifying their position. Constable Campbell-Waugh insists there was no strip search, even though the Nova Scotia Court of Appeal, in striking down the original ruling, said that the search met the legal definition of a strip search. Jones and Derrick maintain that they were not calling Campbell-Waugh a racist but were drawing attention to the systemic racism that still remains entrenched in too many of Canada's institutions.

One way to create Canada is to change laws, to make them more just and relevant to the lives of real people. Rocky Jones and his legal associates had the courage to persevere through a lengthy and costly case that, had they lost, would have set back the cause of freedom of expression under the Charter.

But the challenges never end. Rocky Jones is still calling on all levels of government to set the parameters for reparations to Black people. "We need an acknowledgement of the past abuses that have occurred, and a commitment from government to end this ongoing abuse," Jones told a 2001 symposium. "We need to be restored to the position in society that we would have occupied had the theft [of dignity and identity] not occurred."

There are already precedents in which Canada has taken steps to right past wrongs. Financial settlements have been made with Japanese dispossessed during World War II. We struggle as a country to right the wrongs perpetuated against Aboriginal peoples. Grievances from Sikhs, Chinese, Ukrainians, Italians and others have also come forward.

There is no doubt that Rocky Jones will persist in finding ways to redress injustices to Black people in Canada, some of whom came here as slaves while others have had to struggle through second-class-citizen status.

CHAPTER SEVEN

THE CARIBBEAN INVASION

F ew Canadians today know or care to remember that it was John George Diefenbaker, the much-caricatured prime minister of Canada from 1957 to 1963, who changed the face of Canada. If Bill Clinton was recognized as the first "Black" president of the U.S.A., John Diefenbaker could be portrayed as Canada's first "Black" prime minister. As a young journalist, I covered the 1957 and 1958 federal elections in which "Dief the Chief" converted a minority government into the largest majority in Canadian political history to that time. When I interviewed him for the Montreal Radio station CFCF during the 1958 campaign, his passion was both infectious and inflammatory. His campaign skills became legendary. Besides his soaring oratory, he had an uncanny ability to remember names. Years later, in the early 1960s, I encountered him on the main street of Prince Albert, Saskatchewan. To my astonishment, he not only remembered me, but he also knew my name.

Diefenbaker ended 22 years of Liberal government, winning a minority in the June 10, 1957 election, edging the Louis St. Laurent's Liberals 111 to 104, with other parties, including the CCF and Social Credit holding the balance of power with 40 seats. With the wind in his sails, Diefenbaker called a snap election for March 31, 1958, and romped to the largest majority government (by percentage of seats) in Canadian history. The Conservatives won 208 of 265 seats, reducing the Liberals, led by Lester Pearson, to a rump of 48 seats.

Diefenbaker, the maverick from Prince Albert, was arguably the strongest proponent of human rights ever to occupy the role of prime minister of Canada. It's worrisome that contemporary history does not recognize a stream of accomplishments that literally changed the face of the country. He is remembered in anger as the man who killed the Avro Arrow, and, in caricature, as the man President Kennedy called "Diefenbawker." In Quebec, journalists, myself among them, called him "Diefenboulanger" and made much of the so-called Diefenbaker/Duplessis Axis in which the dictatorial Quebec premier threw the powerful Union National political machine into the election on the side of the Conservatives. One of my broadcasting colleagues, also an engineer, was commissioned to build a special podium for "the Chief," containing a hidden tape recorder. Diefenbaker's French was atrocious. He pre-recorded parts of his speeches in phonetic French, and when speaking in Quebec, would turn on the tape recorder and lip-synch a few words in French. It fooled no one.

But it was Diefenbaker who first gave Aboriginal Canadians the right to vote. In 1958, soon after forming a majority government, he fulfilled a campaign promise by appointing the first Aboriginal member of the Senate—James Gladstone, a respected elder of the Blood First Nation and founder of the Indian Association of Alberta. Diefenbaker appointed Ellen Fairclough, the first woman cabinet minister in Canadian history, and Paul Yuzyk, the first Ukrainian Canadian cabinet minister. Diefenbaker also welcomed the first Chinese Canadian into his caucus, as well as recommending the appointment of George Vanier, the first francophone Governor General. During World War II, Diefenbaker was one of the few who argued against the internment of Japanese Canadians. He led the fight against apartheid in South Africa, which eventually led to the country being expelled from the British Commonwealth. Long before the idea of multiculturalism entered the Canadian dialogue, Diefenbaker was an earnest and committed practitioner.

Diefenbaker opposed the West Indian Domestic Scheme, created by the government of Louis St. Laurent in 1955. The policy allowed unmarried Black women between the ages of 18 and 35, with no family ties and in "good health," to enter Canada as maids. It allowed 100 domestics into the country annually. After one year, the women could apply for landed immigrant status. At first, the scheme was open only to women from Jamaica and Barbados, but it was later expanded to include domestics from other Caribbean islands. Today, a version of the policy that still applies to Filipina women is under attack. In the time of "Uncle Louie," as St. Laurent was known, the policy was considered to be progressive by mainstream Canada.

Diefenbaker's attempts to bring forward a Bill of Rights that would be integrated into a new constitution ran into procedural and ideological opposition. He vowed to protect rights "defined and guaranteed in precise and practical terms to all men by the law of the land." His 1960 Canadian Bill of Rights, passed as an act of parliament and adopted unanimously in August 1960, is a milestone that few Canadians remember or celebrate. Diefenbaker saw the bill as a first step.

Speaking on the CBC program, *The Nation's Business* on June 30, 1960, he said:

> The hallmark of freedom is recognition of the sacred personality of man, and its acceptance decries discrimination on the basis of race, creed or colour. Canadians have a message to give to the world. We are composed of many racial groups, each of which must realize that only by forbearance and mutual respect, only by denial of antagonisms of prejudice based on race, or creed, or even surname, can breaches in unity be avoided in our country.

Diefenbaker was particularly sensitive to the way his name was treated as foreign and undesirable by some people. He told the House of Commons, "I know something of what it has meant in the past for some to regard those with names of other than British or French origin as not being that kind of Canadian that those of British or French origin could claim to be."

The Bill of Rights did not have the teeth that many wished for, but it set the stage for Pierre Trudeau, more than two decades later, to create the Canadian Charter of Rights and Freedoms as part of a new constitution finally brought home to Canada from Britain. Diefenbaker regarded the Bill of Rights as his outstanding achievement, but it was the changes his government made to the regulations governing immigration that dramatically opened the doors to the creation of the multicultural society we are today.

Before Diefenbaker came to power in 1957, immigration to Canada was severely restricted. The Chinese Exclusion Act, which prohibited immigration from China, an ugly law that followed the imposition of a head tax on Chinese immigrants that rose from $50 to $500, was not repealed until 1947. Government policy was geared to preserving Canada, in the words of Prime Minister Mackenzie King and many other politicians of his era, as a "white man's country." Immigrants from the old white Commonwealth, the United States and certain European countries were sought and welcomed. All others were rebuffed.

On January 19, 1962, Diefenbaker's minister of citizenship and immigration, Ellen Fairclough, tabled a new set of regulations in the House of Commons. Henceforth immigrants would not be admitted or denied because of where they came from or what they looked like, but on what skills and education they brought to the country. Race and country of origin were taken out of the equation. Immigrants had to have a job waiting for them or the ability to support themselves until they found one, and they had to be free of diseases that might endanger public health. Criminals or terrorists, then as now, were excluded. Canada, way ahead of the U.S. and Australia, was the first country to liberalize its immigration laws.

New, even more liberal regulations were adopted in 1967 by the Liberal government of Lester Pearson. They introduced a point system that recognized factors like education, age and fluency in English or French, and took into account employment opportunities in Canada. The regulations specifically eliminated nationality or race as criteria and allowed visitors to apply for immigrant status while in Canada. Also brought into play was the Family Reunification program. It allowed women who had come to serve wealthy Montrealers and Torontonians as domestics in the 1950s to finally bring their families to join them.

And so began the Caribbean invasion. The complexion of the country was about to change. In 1966, 87 percent of immigrants to Canada came from Europe. By 1970, 50 percent came from the West Indies, Haiti, Guyana, India, Hong Kong, the Philippines and Indochina. Today, with some 5.5 million citizens in greater Toronto, the area is ranked as one of the most multicultural in the world and is on its way to a future in which visible minorities will become the majority.

According to the 2006 census, 46.9 percent of the city's population was made up of visible minorities. Black citizens represent 8.4 percent of the population (208,555) and were the third largest visible minority group. The largest group were South Asians, representing 12 percent of the population (298,370), and the Chinese come in second, with 283,075 people representing 11.4 percent of the population. In an interesting and growing trend, some 31,100 Torontonians claim multiple visible minority roots. Half of the city's residents were born in another country. In the 21st century, the children of mixed-race couples, with interesting eyes and wonderful hair, are becoming a new and noticeable demographic.

The Right Honourable John George Diefenbaker should be lauded as one of our greatest champions of human and minority rights. Canadians, especially

Black Canadians, owe a debt of gratitude to the 13th prime minister of Canada.

Thanks to Dief the Chief.

THE JAMAICANS

The first West Indians to come to Canada were Jamaicans who landed in Nova Scotia early in our country's history. It's worth noting that slaves brought to North America had varying experiences under different regimes. Those who came to mainland America suffered the well-known ordeals that animate the U.S.A.'s political and social discourse to this day. Those who were sold into the West Indian islands under British, Spanish and French rule generally had less harsh experiences.

In Jamaica, substantial numbers of determined slaves were able to run away from their owners and create their own free communities in the mountains of the island's interior. Known as the Maroons, they were proud, independent and ready to fight for their freedom. In 1795 they launched the second of two wars against the British who, unable to win by military means, attempted to solve the problem by offering freedom in Nova Scotia. There is some question as to whether the Jamaicans were captured and deported or whether they moved north of their own free will. In any event, the first large group, more than 500 strong, arrived in Halifax in 1796 and were offered work building and fortifying the Halifax Citadel.

But the freedom that was promised in Canada did not materialize. Feeling betrayed by the British, the Maroons negotiated arrangements to return to Africa. In 1800, a large group set sail for Sierra Leone and landed at an area they called Freetown. As it happens, some did not make the transition to life in Africa and returned to Jamaica. Some stuck it out in Canada; however, and many Black Nova Scotians trace their ancestry to this brave contingent.

But the largest wave of Caribbean immigrants to Canada, led by a later generation of Jamaicans, didn't take place until the second half of the 20th century. Immigrants from many other West Indian island states were part of a wave that began in earnest in the 1970s and grew in volume through the '80s and '90s and into the 21st century.

But most came from Jamaica. Perhaps it was the bold blood of the Maroons flowing through the veins of their descendents that impelled them to seek a better life and to fight for freedom wherever they were. Jamaicans in Toronto created strong community organizations. When Jamaica won its independence from Britain in 1962, a group of expatriates gathered in Toronto to celebrate the occasion and created the Jamaican Canadian Association.

As the Black population of Toronto increased through the 1970s and into the '90s, West Indian immigrants were increasingly seen as a threat to the larger community. The focus of organizations like the Jamaican Canadian Association morphed from their primary role of providing community and immigrant services to lobbying against a rising tide of discrimination in housing, employment, policing and public services.

Interestingly, the association also provided education in English as a second language. Although English was the official language of the former British colony, many immigrants arrived speaking only the colourful dialect that is the most common means of communication among working-class Jamaicans. Jamaicans have had a powerful impact on Toronto's mainstream culture, with the music of Bob Marley and the Wailers, Culture, The Mighty Diamonds, Shaggy, Mutabaruka, Burning Spear and others in a new generation of artists animating the airways and nightclubs. Restaurants and grocery stores offering island specialties such as plantains, ackee and saltfish, rice and peas, jerk chicken, fish and pork, curried goat, pepperpot soup, roasted yams, banana fritters, patties, exotic desserts and other foods can be found throughout the Greater Toronto Area (GTA).

Is your mouth watering?

BROMLEY LLOYD ARMSTRONG

The fact that the Canada of today is a more tolerant and civic society is in no small part as a result of Bromley's determination to fight racism in all of its manifestations.

–R. Roy McMurtry, Chief Justice of Ontario, 2000

Bromley Armstrong was in the vanguard of post-war immigration from Jamaica. He arrived in Canada in 1947, already toughened by experiences as a union member in Jamaica and encounters with racism in the United States. He was one of the first Jamaicans to take a leadership role in using the law to fight discrimination in our country. He was born in Kingston on February 9, 1926, into a family in which his mother, a midwife, was the principal breadwinner. His father, Eric, a boilermaker and welder more often unemployed than employed, was nevertheless a strong influence. Both a strong unionist and, according to his eldest son, also named Bromley, "a nut for physical culture," the senior Bromley was the middle of seven children. He and a younger brother became successful boxers, but a concussion received in a bout against a much heavier opponent ended Bromley's boxing career.

When he was 16, Bromley decided to leave school. "With my father's influence," he said, "I too became a blood and guts sympathizer within the ranks of the union movement." He went to work for a dry goods merchant and joined Jamaica's Trade Union Congress and learned about the trials and tribulations facing local workers. But he was itching to leave Jamaica. Two older brothers had managed to immigrate to Canada through one of the few means available (except for students or women who could come as domestic workers) at the time. The brothers joined the Canadian Army during World War II, and as British subjects, were allowed to settle in Canada. Once settled, the brothers enrolled Bromley as a student at the Toronto Business College.

It wasn't long before Bromley became involved in the Toronto union movement. He held a relatively menial job at the Massey Harris factory while taking a course in welding at night school. He joined the United Auto Workers Local and was soon elected shop steward, later holding a number of key leadership positions, including a role as auditor and member of the union's fair practices committee. He was actively involved in the formation and leadership of a number of organizations, including the Universal Negro Improvement Association, the Negro Citizenship Association and the Jamaican Canadian Association. He was the youngest member of a 1954 delegation that went to Ottawa to try to persuade the government of Louis St. Laurent to loosen immigration laws that discriminated against people of colour.

As vice president of the Toronto United Negro Credit Union from 1950 to 1954, he helped promote economic independence within the Black community. He extended the reach of his advocacy role by publishing a newspaper, the *Islander*, during the 1970s. In 1975, Bromley Armstrong was a founding member of the Urban Alliance on Race Relations in Toronto, with a mandate to "promote a stable and healthy multiracial environment in the community." He served as a member of the Ontario Human Rights Commission from 1975 to 1980 and was a member of the 1972 Advisory Council on Multiculturalism.

Armstrong was among those who lobbied the Ontario government of Leslie Frost to bring in legislation against discrimination in accommodation and public services. He had personally tested the range of discrimination in housing in Toronto. Along with a Chinese Canadian University of Toronto student, Bromley responded to ads offering rooms or apartments for rent. They were told that the premises had already been rented. But when a white couple who was part of their team followed up on the same ads, they, of course, were welcomed. The team built similar cases with visits to restaurants and the so-called private clubs of the day. On one occasion, Armstrong demanded to be served in a restaurant and kept his cool even while the owner brandished a meat cleaver.

The Fair Employment Practices Act and its companion, the Fair Accommodation Practices Act, were enacted in 1954. The Fair Accommodation Practices Act stated: "No one can deny to any person or class of persons the accommodation, services or facilities usually available to members of the public."

Bromley and his team were the first to test the legislation. The group included Hugh Burnett, an activist carpenter based in Dresden, Ontario, and Donna Hill, wife of human rights activist Daniel Hill, and mother to author Lawrence and musician Dan.

The town of Dresden, a community that had become home to many former American slaves, including Josiah Henson who came to Canada via the Underground Railway, had developed an anti-Black reputation. Bromley's group staged sit-ins in restaurants, barbershops and other businesses that refused to serve minorities. The evidence they gathered was brought to the government, which, true to the intent of its legislation, prosecuted the owners of the premises and won. It was the first successful test of anti-discrimination laws in Canada.

Bromley Lloyd Armstrong's achievements have been well recognized. He is a member of both the Order of Ontario and the Order of Canada. Among many other honours, he has received the Jamaican Order of Distinction, the Canadian Labour Congress' Humanitarian Award, the Stanley Knowles Humanitarian Award, the Baha'i National Race Unity Award and Harmony Award and the Harry Jerome Award. His biography, *Bromley: Tireless Champion for Just Causes*, was co-written with Dr. Sheldon Taylor, a Toronto-based scholar and author of many works on human rights, with an introduction by Mr. Justice Roy McMurtry.

Few Black activists could match the tireless dedication of Bromley Armstrong to the cause of racial equality. As of this writing, he is in his 80s and is still a powerful spokes-person for Black causes.

ROSEMARY WEDDERBURN BROWN

Another child of Jamaica who has made a magnifi-cent contribution to the creation of Canada was human rights activist Rosemary Brown. Rosemary Wedderburn came to Canada as a student, enrolling at McGill University in Montreal in 1950. Born in Kingston, Jamaica, on June 17, 1930, into a matriarchal, well-educated and relatively affluent family, she grew up in a protected environment, well shielded from prejudice and discrimination by her mother, her grandmother and assorted aunts. So it came as a shock to her when, as a 20-year-old, she moved into the Royal Victoria College, the women's residence at McGill. In an environment in which students traditionally doubled up into shared liv-ing quarters, no white student would room with her. She was assigned one of the few single rooms, but it was no consolation. Equally distressing was the reality that few white students would sit with her in the school cafeteria, ignoring her if she joined their table. When she moved out of residence, she encountered the even more blatant experience of white landlords who would simply refuse, without any hint of subtlety, to rent to anyone who was not white.

But as she reported in her biography, *Being Brown*:

> My childhood had prepared me better than I realized to deal with prejudice. Unlike Black Americans and Black Canadians, I did not become a member of a racial minority group until I was an adult with a formed sense of myself. By then it was too late to imprint on me the term "inferior." I knew that all the things that we were told Blacks could

not do, all the jobs that were closed to us in this country, were in fact being done ably, competently and sometimes in a superior way by Blacks at home [in Jamaica] and in other parts of the world.

Rosemary's story is, among other things, a testament to the importance of childhood upbringing. Some of the people portrayed in this book, almost miraculously, triumphed over the soul-shrinking experiences of slavery and other forms of racism to carve out lives that set glowing examples for others. But many others started life in families whose parents gave them strong, positive self-images that led them to inevitably challenge the stereotypes of racial inferiority that still prevail, albeit in increasingly subtle and systemic forms.

It was almost inevitable that throughout her life, Rosemary Wedderburn Brown became a champion of human rights, of women's issues and of political democracy. Her older brother, Hobartson Augustus James Wedderburn, known to his friends as Gus, was a lawyer and activist who played a significant role in the fight against discrimination in Nova Scotia. Rosemary was greatly influenced by Betty Friedan's *The Feminine Mystique*, commenting in her autobiography that it "was one of the three 'jolts' that have hardened my commitment to feminism; the other two were Marilyn French's *The Women's Room*, a book about the sometimes brutal relationship between men and women, and a strange little TV drama called *The Stepford Wives*..."

Rosemary graduated from McGill in 1955, married fellow student, William (Bill) Theophlus Brown, and worked to help put him through medical school. Bill Brown became a successful physician and psychiatrist, and the couple shared a solid, lifelong partnership. They moved to Vancouver where Rosemary completed a Master of Social Work degree at the University of British Columbia and began a career as a social worker and a counsellor at Simon Fraser University. She immersed herself in social issues of the era and became the ombudswoman and a founder of the Vancouver Status of Women Council.

Rosemary was a member of the British Columbia Association for the Advancement of Coloured People (BCAAP) and of the Voice of Women. She had, by this time, proven herself to be both a dynamic speaker and motivator and a superlative organizer. For a time in the 1960s, in her role as a social worker, she appeared on *People in Conflict,* a national weekly television program. She addressed international conferences in Australia, Sweden, Denmark, Greece, Nigeria, the United States, and, of course, throughout the Caribbean.

In 1972, friends prevailed upon her to run for public office. She ran with little expectation of winning but was elected to the British Columbia Legislature, the first Black woman in Canada to be elected to legislative office. She served in the Legislature until her retirement from elected politics in 1986. In 1975, again at the urging of friends, she became the first woman to run for the leadership of a federal political party. On the fourth ballot at the New Democratic Party convention, she lost, narrowly, to Ed Broadbent, who went on to lead the party from 1975 to 1989.

While a member of BC's NDP government, Rosemary Brown led a number of initiatives that contributed to the Canada we know today. She launched a committee to eliminate sexism in school curricula and in textbooks. She also introduced legislation against discrimination on the basis of sex or marital status and was instrumental in the establishment of the Royal Commission on Family and Children's Law, led by the well-known judge, the Hon. Thomas R. Berger, O.C., Q.C. The commission's report, among other things, promoted equality between spouses. As a direct result of her efforts, more women in BC were appointed to boards, commissions and other public bodies.

Life after politics did not slow Rosemary down. Rather, she lived an increasingly involved life. In 1987 she became a professor of Women's Studies at Simon Fraser University. From 1989 to 1993, she served as the executive director of the Match International Centre in Ottawa, a role she considered very important. Match supports programs for women and children worldwide and sponsors several programs in African countries. Match International's mission works in three areas: women and sustainable human development, violence against women and emerging issues focusing primarily on HIV/AIDS. She left Match to take up a three-year term as chief commissioner of the Ontario Human Rights Commission.

In addition, Rosemary served on a wide variety of boards of directors, including the Canadian Security Intelligence Review Committee, the Global Fund for Women, the Canadian Auto Workers Social Justice Fund, Queen's University and Vision TV, Canada's Faith Network. She was a founding member of the Canadian Women's Foundation and a member of the Institute of Public Affairs at Dalhousie University and the Judicial Council of BC.

And as if all of these roles weren't enough, she developed growing status as a writer, with regular columns published in the *Vancouver Sun* and *Herizons,* as well as penning her autobiography, *Being Brown,* which also was published in a children's version.

Rosemary Brown was recognized with a 1973 United Nations Human Rights Fellowship. In 1995 she was inducted into the Order of British Columbia and, in 1996, became an officer of the Order of Canada. In addition to the Order of Jamaica, she received honorary degrees from the University of Toronto, the University of British Columbia, McGill University and a dozen others. She was a member of the Privy Council of Canada and of the Order of Canada Advisory Committee.

Rosemary Wedderburn Brown died in her sleep at home in Vancouver in 2003. A National Film Board documentary, *For Jackson: A Time Capsule from His Two Grandmothers,* chronicles the life of Rosemary Brown and Ruth Horricks-Sujir, both of whom are grandmothers to Jackson.

In one of many columns that celebrated Brown's life, journalist Michelle Landsberg wrote:

FAREWELL TO A POLITICAL KUNG FU FIGHTER

Sometimes a person's life is so rich and various in accomplishment, friendships, small kindnesses and far-flung commitments that only when that life is ended do all the pieces finally slide into one coherent picture. It's like that with Rosemary Brown, who died unexpectedly in her sleep on April 26 at the age of 72. The pieces of her life make a fantastic mosaic that seems to grow brighter as we all begin to grasp the depth and breadth of her contribution.

But perhaps it was Rosemary Brown herself who best summed up her life in her autobiography: "I find it difficult to imagine a time when I will ever be able to turn my back on any struggle for dignity and human rights anywhere."

BRANDEIS DENHAM JOLLY

Like Rosemary Brown, Denham Jolly came to Canada as a student well ahead of the larger migrations from Jamaica in the '60s and '70s. He was born on August 26, 1935, at Industry Cove (now known as Green Island) in Jamaica. On the day he was born, the British governor of the island, Sir Edward Brandeis Denham, was passing through town, and Jolly's mother, sensing that the second of her five children would become a leading citizen, named him Brandeis Denham.

Jolly arrived in Canada in 1955, breaking through the restrictions of the era as a brilliant student with a McGill University scholarship. It should be noted that Canada's door was often open to brilliant scholarship students from the British Caribbean. The award-winning author Austin Clarke came from Barbados as a student to the University of Toronto in 1955. My father, Felix Paul Blache-Fraser, came to Montreal from Trinidad in the 1920s as a scholarship student to study law at McGill University.

Jolly graduated with a Bachelor of Science degree and went home to work on nutrition research for the Government of Jamaica. But like many other West Indians educated in the U.S., Britain or Canada who intended to return home to help their people, the lure of the more advanced countries, in contrast to continuing poverty in the homeland, was hard to resist. Jolly returned to Canada and worked on air pollution research for Metro Toronto. He soon earned an Ontario High School Teaching Certificate and for seven years taught chemistry and physics at the prestigious Forest Hills Collegiate, in the heart of what was then Toronto's upper-class Jewish enclave.

An entrepreneur at heart, Jolly decided that the best way to solve his own need for housing was to buy a property and turn it into a rooming house. He collected rent from his tenants and lived in the most modest room in the house. It wasn't long before he was investing in properties around the GTA and beyond and turning good profits. His investments included a Day's Inn hotel in west Toronto, a nursing home in Texas, two medical laboratories and the Tyndal Nursing Home in Mississauga, which, at this writing, he still owns.

But it wasn't only his skills as a businessman that make Jolly an important contributor to Canada's business sector. As a fierce take-no-prisoners advocate for Black causes, he encountered his own share of discrimination. He fought his way through the attitudes of banks that were reluctant to provide loans for his enterprises by proving over and over that he could exceed their expectations, succeeding in business and more than meeting his obligations.

In an incident that rankles him to this day, he was deeply insulted when a white man saw him about to enter a whirlpool bath at the Central Toronto YMCA. At the time, Jolly was a member of the prestigious board of directors of the "Y." The man asked Jolly, sneeringly, if he had taken a shower to cleanse himself before entering the pool. Jolly still shakes with rage when he recounts the story. His hostile response ensured that the man would never make that mistake again.

One of Denham Jolly's most important early achievements was the creation of the Black Business and Professional Association (BBPA). On October 21, 1982,

Jolly invited about 25 people to the Underground Railroad, a popular downtown Toronto restaurant operated by blues singer Salome Bey and her husband Howard Mathews. The attendees were a who's who of prominent people in the Black community; among them was Bromley Armstrong; journalist Al Hamilton; television broadcaster Hamlin Grange; lawyer and later judge Romain Pitt; citizenship court judge Pamela Appelt; educator Jean Augustine; Jean Gammage (Kamala-Jean Gopie), a member of the Ontario Advisory Council on Multiculturalism and Citizenship; and CBC journalist, Cynthia Reyes. Jolly was acclaimed as the BBPA's first president.

The association's first convention was scheduled for March 5, 1983. Included in the plan was a series of awards and scholarships that recognized and supported Black achievement. Jolly invited Vancouver-based runner Harry Jerome, who, during the 1960s was the fastest man in the world, to give the keynote address. Tragically, Jerome died of a seizure on December 7, 1982. He was 42. One of Canada's most outstanding athletes, Jerome competed in three Olympic games and held six world track records. He was a member of the Order of Canada and has a star on the Canadian Walk of Fame in Toronto's theatre district. It was Hamlin Grange who suggested the awards be named for Harry Jerome.

The Harry Jerome Awards, the most prestigious event of its kind in Canada, has since been held annually in Toronto every spring. The Harry Jerome Scholarship Fund was established in 1988. With as many as 1000 men and women in formal wear in attendance, the Harry Jerome Awards is a glittering gala regularly attended by prime ministers, provincial premiers, mayors and other dignitaries.

Denham Jolly, with immense energy and commitment, threw himself into Black community affairs at many levels. He was an active member of the Jamaican Canadian Association, the Black Action Defence Committee, the Committee for Due Process, the Daphne Dacosta Cancer Association, the Jane Finch Concerned Citizens Movement, the Black Inmates Organization and the Harriett Tubman Games as well as the YMCA. He made substantial contributions to Caribana, Toronto's famous West Indian–inspired Carnival, which attracts thousands of spectators and is considered one of the city's major tourist attractions. Unknown to the wider world, Jolly's quiet acts of philanthropy, helping a student with tuition here, supporting a struggling entrepreneur there, have changed the lives of many.

In 1982, Toronto's Black community needed a voice through which it could express its concerns and report on events ignored by mainstream media. Jolly's fighting spirit drew him to the cause. He was the publisher and financial backer of a weekly newspaper, *Contrast,* which quickly became the medium of record for Black events in the GTA.

But an even louder voice was needed, one that reflected the culture of Toronto's Black citizens, that played its music, that celebrated and created its stars and that brought news of events important to the minority community. In one of the most richly served media markets in the country, they needed a radio station. A number of prominent citizens joined Jolly in his application for a broadcast licence. Zanana Akande, Carl Redhead, Reynold Austin and Tony Davy became shareholders in Milestone Radio, Inc. (Readers should be aware that I am an outside [none shareholding] board member of the

Milestone Radio.) However, it took several frustrating attempts for the radio station to succeed.

Jolly's application for an urban music radio licence was opposed by the broadcasting community and rebuffed by the Canadian Radio-television and Telecommunications Commission (CRTC). His first application in 1990 was passed over in favour of a country music station. A second attempt in 1997 was thwarted when the CRTC gave the 99.1 FM frequency to the CBC. Many observers considered the decision to have racist undertones. Toronto did not have an urban music station; the CBC simply wanted an FM frequency for its Radio One service, already available on AM 740.

It was only after Jolly persuaded an established mainstream broadcaster to take a minority share in the enterprise that the CRTC, in 2000, finally granted him a licence on a low penetration channel. Flow 93.5 went on the air on February 9, 2001. Subsequent increasing in power allowed the station to reach audiences throughout the GTA, permitting it to become a major player in the country's richest broadcasting market. The station was and is the first and only Black-owned radio station in Canada. In 2004, Milestone Radio in partnership with CHUM, one of the oldest radio broadcasters in Toronto, applied for and received a licence to operate a radio station in Edmonton. Known as The Bounce, the new station went on the air on February 17, 2005, and, like its Toronto counterpart, is near the top of the charts in the local radio spectrum.

Denham Jolly, through his broadcasting operations, has changed the nature of urban radio in this country. His early sponsorship of Black organizations and causes made tangible contributions to the ability of Blacks to participate in the creation of Canada.

DONOVAN BAILEY

To Canadians at large, Donovan Bailey is probably the best-known Jamaican immigrant. In 1995 he was the first to break the 10-second barrier for the 100-metre sprint first established by Harry Jerome in 1960, inheriting the title as the world's fastest human.

Born in Manchester, Jamaica, on December 16, 1967, Bailey came to Canada when he was 13. He played basketball and competed in track and field at Queen Elizabeth Park High School in Oakville, Ontario. But in earning a degree in business administration at Sheridan College, he discovered that he had a flair for entrepreneurship. He nevertheless continued competing successfully in athletics sprint events on a part-time basis through the early 1990s. He was a successful stockbroker in 1994 when he decided to get serious about running and began training for the 1995 World Track and Field Championships in Sweden. Already in his late 20s, an age when most sprinters have hung up their track shoes, he surprised the world by winning the 100-metre sprint and anchoring the team that won the 4×100 relay.

Many Canadians will remember his extraordinary triumph on July 27, 1996, at the Atlanta Olympics when he won the 100-metre sprint with a world record time of 9.84 seconds. The Olympic record stood until Maurice Greene broke the record in 1999. Bailey's career effectively ended when he ruptured his Achilles tendon during the 1998 season. He tried to make a comeback at the 2000 Olympics, but illness prevented him from reaching the finals. He retired in 2001, having been a five-time World and Olympic champion.

Since then, Bailey has become a highly successful businessman and a much sought-after motivational speaker.

Bailey Inc. has real estate holdings, a clothing business and a sports training centre. One of his companies, DBX Sport Management, works with both amateur and professional athletes.

Donovan Bailey is a member of the Canadian Sports Hall of Fame.

THE TRINIDADIANS

Something that many mainstream Canadians still don't "get" is the deep-rooted *joi de vivre* of Caribbean people. American Blacks with roots corroded by slavery developed deep religious beliefs to help them through their ordeals and revelled in the powerful gospel music that came with it. However, island people, with what seems like a lighter touch, embraced a love of life that expressed itself in music and dance, and above all, the celebration of annual pre-Lent festivals, the greatest of which is the Trinidadian Carnival.

Like Jamaica, Trinidad and Tobago (T&T) gained its independence from Britain in 1962. It is arguably the most multicultural of the island nations. Its population includes remnants of the Aboriginal Carib "Indians," decimated by the Europeans and the diseases they brought when Columbus arrived in 1492. Before it became part of the British Empire, T&T had been under the control of the Spanish and the French, who have also contributed to the cultural mix. Africans were brought as slaves, and in the 1840s, Indian Hindus and Muslims were offered free passage to the islands in return for five years of indentured service at a fixed wage. People with Chinese roots also found their way to the islands.

Today, descendants of Africans and East Indians make up the bulk of the population of T&T. With a majority made up of what we call visible minorities, racial discrimination of the type encountered in North America is, for all practical purposes, nonexistent. That lack of tension probably accounts, at least in part, for the celebration of Carnival. The playful music of calypso and the invention of the steel drum or pan as a musical instrument are T&T innovations. The pan is considered to be the only bona fide acoustical musical instrument invented in the 20th century.

There are steel pan orchestras in Port of Spain that specialize in classical music. In the 1950s and '60s, Lord Caressa, a former Trinidadian, held sway at several Montreal nightclubs. His genius, the essence of calypso music, was to invent lyrics about someone in the audience and, on the spot, weave it into a song. I well remember attending his performances at a popular St. Catherine Street nightclub. He and another Trinidadian, Lord Kitchener (many calypsonians affected royal names) popularized West Indian music in the city.

CARNIVAL

With its spectacularly colourful annual celebrations, Carnival is one of the great West Indian contributions to Canadian culture. The festivals, which have their strongest roots in Trinidad and Tobago, spread across the Caribbean as well as across Canada. Caribana, the largest of the festivals, is held in Toronto and is one of the city's major tourist attractions. It began in 1967 as part of Canada's centennial celebration, a gift from proud Caribbean Canadians to their new country.

Carnival has both pagan and religious roots. Some say that the idea goes back to the Saturnalia of the Christian Romans. Lent, a 40-day period of symbolic penitence leading up to Easter, during which Christians are expected to lead a near Spartan life, giving up some or all of the nonessential pleasures of life, also yielded to the continuation of ancient pagan spring rites. In a bow to their inexpugnable persistence, the early Church allowed its followers a pre-Lent period during which the strict bonds of proprietary were loosened and normal restraints were relaxed if not altogether abandoned. The oldest expression of the idea in North America is the famous New Orleans Mardi Gras ("fat Tuesday" before Ash Wednesday), which has been celebrated since 1827 and during which, according to reports, anything goes. In their Canadian expression, Carnivals are not connected to Lent. An outdoor festival in pre-Easter weather is not even close to practical. Our Carnivals are sensibly held in summer and attract the whole multicultural crowd, with people of all backgrounds dancing along in the parade. Edmontonians delighted in seeing Michael Phair, a diminutive, long-standing white member of City Council, dressed in an outlandishly colourful outfit, doing a "jump up" dance along the parade route.

Hundreds of thousands of tourists come to see the parade that travels along the Toronto lakeshore. It is celebrated as the largest street festival in North America. As many as 1.3 million visitors annually take in the two-week event, which begins in mid-July and culminates on the August civic holiday, pumping as much as $250 million into the city's economy.

But other Canadian cities also have their own carnivals: Montreal has its Carifiesta; Edmonton's Cariwest is mirrored by Calgary's Carifest; Winnipeg has Caripeg; Ottawa celebrates Caribe-Expo; Caribbean Days are celebrated in North Vancouver; and Hamilton hosts an annual Mardi Gras Carnival. Though smaller than the Toronto carnival, each has become a major annual event drawing thousands of spectators and participants. Many of the festival's features—steel pan, calypso and soca music, and popular competitions for the best king and queen costumes—originated in Trinidad and Tobago.

Reggae music from Jamaica reflects the way carnival is celebrated in other island countries such as Barbados, Guyana, St. Vincent, the Bahamas and Antigua. Many cultures come together in the Canadian event. Even contemporary Canadian influences, including popular music, have become part of the festivals.

I was able to see an authentic West Indian carnival firsthand during an early '90s visit to Port of Spain, the capital of Trinidad and Tobago. The event begins with a blast early in the morning of Dimanche Gras (literally "fat Sunday"), also known as "Jou-vay," taken from the French *j'ouvert* (I open). It continues until Shrove Tuesday, the day before the beginning of Lent on Ash Wednesday. I was awakened in my hotel room early on Jou-vay morning with an ear-splitting blast so loud I thought that someone had placed a pair of the biggest, loudest speakers in creation at the foot of my bed. It was the coming out of the bands, a group of spectacularly costumed and masked revellers that can number in the hundreds "playing mas," the colloquial term for participating in Carnival.

At about 4:00 AM on Jou-vay morning, each "band," led by musicians on flatbed 18-wheeler trucks, who play through oversized speakers that sound like they're on steroids, wind their way through the city. In Port of Spain they come down from the hillside communities around the city through the Savanna, a famous down-town park, to the parade grounds where, on the day before Lent, they parade before the carnival's judges. But by sunrise on Jou-vay, the pre-dawn event is over, the bands melt away back to their various camps, and everything is quiet.

Fierce competition between bands is a major feature of Carnival. A band can include hundreds of people who spend months leading up to the event preparing elaborate matched costumes reflecting a particular theme. Band members pay for, and often help to build, their costumes. The exceptions are the competitions for king and queen of Carnival, whose brilliantly extravagant costumes are usually animated and always larger than life. The costumes are worn by robust dancers who are strapped into the creations, some so heavy that their weight has to be carried on wheels. Being crowned the queen and king of the festival is the most coveted prize. Designers spend months on their creations, often starting on next year's plans soon after the current carnival wraps up.

One of the most internationally celebrated Carnival designers is Trinidadian Peter Minshall. A revered artist, he describes his medium as "the mas." Participants in the bands say they "make mas." Minshall likes to be called a "masman." He, perhaps more than anyone, has driven the artistic development of Carnival, both in Port of Spain and in the vibrant Canadian variations. Many Canadians have travelled to Port of Spain to study with him. The year that I attended Carnival, Minshall's costumes for the king and queen of the festival, a pair of six-metre-tall, animated characters, won the prize. The amazingly articulated queen and king of the band, Tan Tan and Saga Boy, are among Minshall's most popular creations—giant puppets that danced with lifelike mannerisms through the streets of Port of Spain.

Minshall, born in Guyana in 1941, moved to Trinidad as a child and was 13 when he made his first carnival costume. Dressed as an African witch doctor, he won the first of many prizes. His fame grew after he graduated from the Central School of Art and Design in London, England. One of the first pinnacles of his career came in 1974 when he designed a carnival costume for his adopted sister, Sherry-Ann Guyto. The costume, called "From the Land of the Hummingbird," took five weeks, a dozen people, 104 feathers, each one made of 150 different pieces of fabric, to craft. It allowed his sister total mobility and its ingenious design soon made it a major icon of the Trinidad carnival. As Minshall's work increased in scope and complexity, photographer Roy Boyke said, "It is doubtful that the work of any single individual has had so searing an impact on the consciousness of an entire country."

Minshall's work has appeared in festivals in Washington, DC; New York City; Miami; San Francisco; London and Paris, as well as in Toronto. My son, Randall Fraser, a theatrical designer and performer, spent several weeks studying with Minshall in Port of Spain before winning the competition for the best costume for the queen of Carnival and best designer at the 2006 Edmonton Cariwest Festival.

Costume makers from festivals in Canada often travelled to Trinidad to study with Minshall, and the results of his influence can be seen on the streets of Toronto, Montreal, Edmonton and Calgary during their carnival festivals.

A costume created by Randall Fraser for Edmonton's Cariwest Festival. The costume, worn by the carnival queen, won best of festival.

A small number of Trinidadians came to Canada in the 1920s to work on the railways or in the shipyards of Nova Scotia. A few came as students and, after getting good educations, stayed as teachers, nurses, civil servants, lawyers, doctors, engineers and artists. But it was only after Diefenbaker's changes to the laws of immigration that they came in substantial numbers. Today, more than 150,000 Canadians trace their origins to T&T, many bringing with them, because of their background, a more profound appreciation of the multiculturalism that Canada is working to embrace.

While about two-thirds of Trinidadians have settled in Toronto and southern Ontario, substantial populations have settled in Montreal, Vancouver, Edmonton and Calgary. Because T&T, like Canada, is an oil- and gas-producing nation, it has a well-developed, educated middle class. A modern-day problem suffered by many immigrants is that T&Ters who arrive with good educations and skills are finding it difficult to acquire work in their fields. There is a strain of systemic discrimination built into Canada's employment system that is reluctant to recognize the training and credentials of immigrants. The result is "downward occupational mobility" that robs Canada of the skills and knowledge it needs.

Nevertheless, many Trinidadian Canadians have succeeded in the arts.

Neil Bissoondath, a nephew of Nobel Prize–winning author V.S. Naipaul, came to Canada in 1973 to study at York University in Toronto. A Governor General's Award nominee, Neil has written several novels, but his book, *Selling Illusions: The Cult of Multiculturalism in Canada*, energized the discussion around how Canada manages its diversity.

Jeff Henry is a talented director, choreographer, actor and teacher, founder of Theatre Fountainhead in Toronto, Director of Movement at the National Theatre School in Montreal, Artist in Residence at the Stratford Festival and a Professor Emeritus and Senior Scholar at York University.

CBC Television anchor Ian Hanomansing was born in Port of Spain, Trinidad, and grew up in Sackville, New Brunswick. He graduated with an honours BA in political science and sociology from Mount Allison University in Sackville, where he was valedictorian. He also has a law degree from Dalhousie University in

Halifax, Nova Scotia. While in university, Hanomansing won six national university debating and public speaking championships.

Ramabai Espinet came to Canada in 1970 and has gained a national reputation as a poet as well as the author of children's and adult fiction. She is a professor at Seneca College in Toronto and has held academic posts at both York University and the University of Toronto.

Another writer with roots in Trinidad and Tobago is Andre Alexis. His parents moved to Canada in 1959, leaving their son and daughter behind in the care of relatives until they were settled. Andre was four when he was reunited with his parents in Ottawa in 1961.

Andre's writing, powerful and evocative, first came to attention with "Despair, and Other Stories of Ottawa," published in 1994. It has been described as "a surreal and macabre depiction of the nation's capital." His first novel, *Childhood,* won the 1997 Books in Canada First Novel Award and shared the prize for the Trillium Award.

BARBADOS

Barbados is another former British colony that has contributed to the Caribbean invasion. It was, according to some perceptions, the most British of the colonies. "Bajans," it is said, are "more British than the British." The tiny island took longer to cut the umbilical cord to Mother England, not winning its independence until 1966, four years after Trinidad and Jamaica had made the break.

An interesting relationship has developed between Barbados and Canada, dating back to 1867, as the

Canadian Confederation was happening. A movement led by the Barbados Agricultural Society, an organization representing the owners of plantations, tried to have the island join Canada. The initiative did not win sufficient support, but the movement stirred anew in the 1960s when Barbados was negotiating its independence. Again, the initiative failed, but over the years many trade and financial ties developed between the two countries. Canadian financial institutions have strong bases on the island, playing a major role in Barbados' economy. In 2008 the three largest Caribbean stock exchanges in Jamaica, Trinidad and Barbados considered the possibility of associating themselves with the Toronto Stock Exchange.

As recently as 2007, Prime Minister Harper expressed an intention to heighten Canada's profile in the Americas. Part of the plan was to negotiate a bilateral free trade and mutual open skies agreement with Barbados. But at this writing, negotiations appear to focus on a Free Trade Agreement between Canada and the CARICOM group of nations, whose members include Barbados.

Some notable Bajans who have contributed to the creation of Canada in various fields are listed below.

AUSTIN ARDINEL CHESTERFIELD CLARKE

His 1980 memoir, *Growing up Stupid Under the Union Jack,* chronicles not only Austin Clarke's own early life but also the overwhelming impact the British education system had on him. Clarke is more widely known for his Giller Prize–winning novel, *The Polished Hoe*, which also won the Commonwealth Writers Prize in 2003. A prolific writer of novels and short stories, he is a bona fide member of the Canadian literary establishment, winning, among many other honours, the Toronto Arts Award for Lifetime Achievement in Literature. Born into a far-from-affluent family in 1934, Clarke displayed a keen intelligence at an early age that was to become his passport to a better life. His very British education gave him the opportunity to embrace the classics of English literature and led to his admittance to Harrison College, the most prestigious boy's school in Barbados.

He came to Canada in 1955 to study economics and political science at Trinity College but soon found that writing was his true calling. With day jobs in broadcasting and print journalism, he began a prolific writing career that included short stories and novels. His most recent novel, *More*, published in 2009, is a contemporary story of a mother who discovers that her son is a member of a criminal gang.

The *Globe and Mail*, in its review of *More*, said, "Clarke brings into the light the dignity and strength with which our mothers and grandmothers have borne their daily exclusions from the more genteel spaces of Canadian identity. By choosing to write Idora's story as Toronto's story, at the height of his literary power, Clarke boldly challenges, and transforms, Canadian sense and sensibility."

For a number of years, Clarke pursued a diplomatic career. In 1974 he was appointed as cultural attaché to the Barbadian Embassy in Washington, DC, later serving as general manager of the Caribbean Broadcasting Corporation in Barbados. But after a couple of years he returned to Canada and committed himself to writing.

Austin Clarke won the prestigious W.O. Mitchell Prize in 1999. He was inducted as a member of the Order of Canada in 1998.

ANNE CLARE COOLS

In 1984, Anne Cools was the first Black to be appointed to the Canadian Senate. She has been a controversial figure on the Canadian political scene since her involvement in a student movement at Sir George Williams University (now Concordia) in 1969. She was part of a sit-in in which students took over one of the university's buildings in a protest against alleged racism at the school. The incident received dramatic television coverage that included shots of students throwing computers out of upper-storey windows. According to reports, some $2 million worth of computer equipment was destroyed. Cools was sentenced to four months in jail for her part in the affair.

Trained as a social worker and ever the crusader, Anne Cools moved to Toronto in 1974 and founded Women in Transition, Inc., one of the first shelters for abused women in Canada. After several unsuccessful attempts to win election to the House of Commons, Cools was appointed to the Senate by Pierre Trudeau. Her career in the Upper House has been no less controversial. Even though she had run for office as a Liberal, she became an outspoken critic of the governments of Jean Chrétien and Paul Martin, and in 2004, she crossed the floor to join the Conservative Party. But in June 2007, she was "read out" of the Conservative Party for her vocal opposition to Prime Minister Stephen Harper. She, among other things, voted against Harper's 2007 budget.

Senator Cools' many accomplishments include extensive work as a member of the Senate/House of Commons Special Joint Committee on Child Custody and Access. In its report, "For the Sake of the Children," the committee recommended shared parenting in the best interests of children in the event of a family breakdown. Cools has been a member of many social advocacy organizations, including the LaMarsh Centre for Research on Violence and Conflict Resolution, the Metro Toronto Justice Committee on Spousal Abuse and the Toronto Black Education Project. Her many honours include *Pride* magazine's Outstanding Achievement Award in Politics in 1997.

Born in 1943, Anne Cools still has many years to serve as a member of the Senate before she reaches the retirement age of 75 in 2018.

WHITFIELD ANDY KNIGHT

One of the most accomplished students to come to Canada from Barbados is Dr. Andy Knight, a professor of political science at the University of Alberta, who, in 2009, was also chair of the department. His path to international acclaim started from a strong artistic base. In fact, those who knew him as a youth would likely have predicted a career in music rather than as a respected participant in the discourse of international politics.

When he was 10, Andy played guitar and piano in a family band (the Knights Brothers) that appeared regularly on a radio program called *Auntie Olga's Children's Show*. Later, he formed a gospel group and sang in choirs throughout Barbados. After coming to Canada in 1977, he played trumpet and piano in high school and landed the role of Nathan Detroit in the school's production of *Guys and Dolls*. Andy also has talent as a visual artist; he says he's been drawing and painting since he was a little boy.

So it should come as no surprise that his first degree, at McMaster University in Hamilton, Ontario, was in fine arts, where he also distinguished himself as the first Black president of the McMaster Students' Union. His work has been featured in art galleries in Hamilton, Halifax, Toronto and Bridgetown, Barbados, and in addition to all of that, he describes himself as a closet fiction writer.

Against that background, it is almost astonishing that Andy Knight would become one of Canada's leading political scientists. Following his undergraduate degree at McMaster, he moved to Halifax to earn a masters degree in political science at Dalhousie University and then to Toronto to earn a PhD in political science at York University. His academic credentials are impressive: he has an affiliate professorship at Landegg International University in Zurich, Switzerland, and an assistant professorship at Bishop University in Quebec.

Since joining the Department of Political Science at the University of Alberta in 1998, his resumé has grown in stature and length. He became a full professor in 2000, filled the prestigious McCalla Research Professorship in 2003–04 and is the Director of Peace and Post Conflict Studies Certificate Program in the Office of Interdisciplinary Studies. He is a leading advocate against the use of children in war and has sponsored a number of conferences and seminars on the issue.

In February 2008, Dr. Knight was appointed by UN Secretary General Ban Ki-Moon to head a new international initiative, the Global Centre for the Responsibility to Protect. His mission was to explore ways in which the international community could intervene in cases where national governments severely abuse their populations. Unfortunately, he had to withdraw in June 2008 for personal and family reasons.

A prolific writer on world affairs, Andy Knight has written an impressive number of papers, academic monographs and books. He is a frequent contributor to the op-ed pages of newspapers ranging from the *Japan Times* to the *Globe and Mail* to the *Edmonton Journal.*

Now in the prime of his life, Andy Knight continues to make unique contributions to the creation of Canada by raising the profile of our country in international journals and agencies.

ANTHONY LINDSAY AUSTIN FIELDS

Another immigrant from Barbados who has distinguished himself in our country is one of Canada's most respected oncologists, Dr. Anthony Fields. He has been president of the National Cancer Institute of Canada and the Canadian Association of Medical Oncologists as well as a member of the Board of Governors of the American College of Physicians, responsible for the Alberta region. He has served as director of Alberta's respected Cross Cancer Institute and currently leads the cancer care program at Alberta health services, at the same time maintaining a professorship at the University of Alberta.

Quite a resumé for a man whose entry into the medical field came relatively late in life and only after a counsellor at the University of Alberta, following a series of vocational tests, told him there was a 95 percent chance that he would succeed as a physician, an idea he says he had never entertained. "[A]t the end of the day, I'm just too old to start medical training," he said. He was 27. The counsellor countered with the information that Dr. Albert Schweitzer was 35 when he entered medical school.

Dr. Anthony Fields accepts the R.M. Taylor Medal and Award of the Canadian Cancer Society and the National Cancer Institute of Canada from Ms. Lori Messer, Toronto, 2007.

Tony Fields was born in Bridgetown, Barbados, on October 21, 1943, into a family that had high expectations for their children. His father, a senior civil servant, and his mother, a teacher, raised four boys, one of whom is a physicist and electronics specialist and another is a biology professor at an American university. So it was part of the family tradition that Tony, the second son, would graduate from the University of Cambridge with an MA in natural sciences and begin a teaching career at

Queen's College in Barbados. But in October 1966, he met an Alberta girl, Patricia Stewart, who was in Barbados as a CUSO (Canadian University Service Overseas) volunteer. They married and moved to Edmonton, where Tony found work as a chemistry technologist in a local steel plant. But Tony's need for higher education was a deeply internalized imperative.

He took the counsellor's advice and entered medical studies at the University of Alberta, following up with further studies at St. Michael's Hospital in Toronto. His intention was to specialize in internal medicine, but an offer of a staff position if he would become a medical oncologist changed his direction. Once on that path, there was no wavering.

Dr. Fields returned to Alberta and rose to become the leading public spokesperson of the Alberta Cancer Board.

In 2006, a patient at the Cross Cancer Institute in Edmonton died because of a mix-up in medication. Within hours of the incident, Dr. Fields addressed the media explaining how the mistake had occurred. He apologized to all concerned, and, as head of the institution, accepted full responsibility for the death—detailing the measures that would be taken immediately to prevent any recurrence. "We are going to use this terrible tragedy as a springboard to become ever safer," said Fields. As vice president of the Alberta Cancer Board, he said the review would also be available to all other cancer centres in Canada. He led a complete overhaul of the methods used to deliver chemotherapy and ensured that the insights gained from the incident were disseminated nationally and internationally.

The family of the deceased woman accepted Dr. Fields' apology and his commitment to changing the system, issuing a statement that they wished "to reassure others that the Cross Cancer Institute remains a place where cancer patients and their families receive world-class care." The nurses who gave the patient the lethal overdose have been cleared of wrongdoing and continue to work at the institute.

Across Canada, editorialists and public relations experts praised Dr. Fields for setting an outstanding example for people in leadership positions. A report on the incident prepared for the Institute for Safe Medication Practices Canada said, "The organization's transparency in its response to the incident and its goal to widely share learning related to the incident analysis demonstrates exceptional leadership."

Dr. Anthony Fields has been honoured in a number of ways. He has twice been named Professor of the Year at the University of Alberta; he was named one of the top 100 physicians of the century in Alberta; and he has been awarded an honorary degree by Athabasca University.

As the spokesperson for the Alberta Cancer Board and as head of the Cross Cancer Institute, Dr. Fields has made a significant contribution to the creation of Canada. In an era where leaders go out of their way to avoid responsibility for failures in the systems they manage, where politicians and bureaucrats and corporate leaders have become expert in passing the buck, Tony Fields has set a new benchmark.

THE HAITIANS

While most immigrants from the Caribbean came to Toronto and points west, it is no surprise that Haitians, whose language is French, came to Quebec. It was a place where more tolerant provisions for refugees and immigration laws made it seem like a promised land to people who found themselves in a French-speaking environment with religious beliefs that reflected their own.

Haiti, the most tumultuous and poverty-stricken of the Caribbean islands, has a heart-breaking history. Following the arrival of Europeans led by Columbus, both Spain and France claimed the island of Hispaniola. The Treaty of Ryswick in 1697 finally settled the issue, awarding the western third of the island to France and establishing what was reputed to be the richest French colony in the New World. The French derived huge profits from a slave-based economy that produced sugar, coffee and indigo for export to France. The Code Noir (Black Code) created by France with the backing of Louis XIV set cruel and rigid rules for slaves. The territory, originally named Saint-Domingue, was one of the most brutal slave colonies in history. One-third of newly arriving slaves were reported to have died within a few years.

After a long and tortured history that included several slave revolutions, Napoleon sent a large force to Saint-Domingue to quell the cry for independence and renamed the territory Haiti, the name for the island used by the indigenous Taino tribe. The country's tumultuous history included a period of occupation, from 1915 to 1934, by the United States. It remains one of the least developed and most politically corrupt countries in the Western Hemisphere. It's no wonder that Haiti's most significant export is its people; refugees escape by any means possible from the brutality of a country that the rest of the world seems impotent to help. There are many reports of would-be immigrants losing their lives after unsafe, overcrowded boats sink as they try to reach U.S. soil.

Many Haitians found refuge in Canada. In 1965 there were only some 2000 Haitians in Quebec. But the ruthless ferocity of the Duvalier regime ("Papa Doc" [François] followed by his son "Baby Doc" [Jean-Claude]) led to a massive exodus of those who could find a way to get out. Some came illegally in boats, many of them not seaworthy, to the United States, eventually forming a substantial community in Florida.

Between 1973 and 1976, some 3000 Haitians came to Canada each year. Statistics Canada records indicate that more than 45,000 immigrated during that period. Another source, the Montreal-based Maison d'Haiti, estimates that 75,000 people with Haitian origins came to Quebec between 1961 and 2006.

A number of distinguished Canadians had their origins in Haiti and a few are listed here.

DANY LAFERRIÈRE

Laferrière's prose is uncompromising. His observation is wicked and sharp. He takes no prisoners, least of all himself.

—*The Irish Press*

Dany Laferrière created a sensation in Quebec literary circles with his 1985 first novel, *Comment faire l'amour avec un Nègre sans se fatiguer*, later translated into English as *How to Make Love to a Negro*. Knowing the value of a good title, Laferrière used the novel to ruminate on the bizarre stereotypes too often linked to Blacks. The book became a screenplay and a movie that was nominated for a Genie (Canada's version of the Oscars) Award in 1990.

Laferrière was born in Port-au-Prince, Haiti, on April 13, 1953, growing up in the village of Petit Goave. He began his working life as a newspaper and radio journalist reporting on cultural issues, something that wasn't easy during the dictatorial Duvalier regime. In 1976, after a colleague with whom he was working on a story was murdered, Laferrière transplanted his journalistic career to Montreal. He hosted a television program on the TQS network, later moving into film as a writer, director and actor.

Laferrière's writing has been prolific and well recognized. His novel *L'Odeur du café (An Aroma of Coffee)* won him le Prix Carbet de la Caraibe in 1991. *Le Gout des jeunes filles* (published in English as *Dining with the Dictator*) brought him the Prix Edgar-Lesperance in 1993. He was awarded the 2002 Prix RFO du Livre for *Cette grenade dans la main du jeune negre est-elle une arme ou un fruit?* (published in English as *Why must a Black Writer Write about Sex?*—a literal translation of the French title, *This Grenade in the Hands of a Young Nigger is a Weapon or a Fruit?*).

His 11th novel, *L'énigme du retour (Puzzles of the Return)*, a tender chronicle of Laferrière's return to Haiti following the death of his father, won the prestigious Prix Médici, awarded by France to an author "whose fame does not yet match their talent."

Many of Laferrière's books have been translated into English as well as Spanish, Korean and Swedish. He currently lives in Montreal but spends part of the year in Miami.

BRUNY SURIN

> Getting to work in the field you want to work in is such luck....It's a privilege. The 100 metres and the 4×100-metre relay have given me a chance to push my limits, to go down into the core of myself to find the strength to achieve my goals.

> —Bruny Surin

Bruny Surin is well remembered by Canadians as a member of the 4×100 relay team that won the gold medal in both the 1994 Commonwealth Games in Victoria, BC, and the 1996 summer Olympics in Atlanta, Georgia.

He moved to Canada in 1975 from Cap-Haïtien, Haiti, where he was born on July 12, 1967. A superb track and field athlete, he first competed for Canada in the 1987 Pan-American Games, placing 15th in the long jump. He competed in the 1988 Seoul, Korea Olympics and achieved the same result, which prompted his coaches to suggest that he give up the long jump in favour of the 100-metre sprint. It was a good decision. The next year Surin won the Canadian championship, running the distance in 10.14 seconds, a fraction off the record set by Harry Jerome when he ran the distance in 10 seconds flat. Surin went on to win bronze in the 100 metres at the 1990 Commonwealth Games in Auckland, New Zealand.

But it was the relay team that continued to win gold—at the 1997 World Championship and the 1998 Goodwill Games. Surin retired from competition to devote himself to a foundation that focuses on the development and promotion of young athletes in Canada.

He was inducted as a member of the Canadian Sports Hall of Fame in 2008.

MICHAËLLE JEAN

[H]ere is this beautiful young Canadian of Haitian birth, with a smile that makes you catch your breath, with a bemused older husband by her side, and a daughter who literally personifies our future, and you look at them and you think: Yes, this is our great achievement, this is the Canada that Canada wants to be, this is the Canada that will ultimately make way for different cultural identities.

–John Ibbitson, *Globe and Mail*, September 28, 2005

Every Canadian knows that the most famous Haitian ever to come to Canada is the Right Honourable Michaëlle Jean, Governor General of Canada. If Barack Obama's story is one that could only have happened in the United States, Michaëlle Jean's story is one that could only happen in Canada. Both individuals have delighted and inspired the majority of their fellow citizens and, at the same time, have provoked profound and sometimes extreme discomfort, among other sentiments. Jean and Obama are at once symbols and harbingers of the sweeping changes taking place in North American society in the 21st century. When they met in Ottawa on February 19, 2009, Jean officially greeted him as the representative of the head of state of Canada, Queen Elizabeth II. It was clear to all observers that the Governor General and the president formed an immediate bond, both delighted with the precedent-setting positions they held, while at the same time fully aware of the challenges ahead.

Michaëlle Jean was born on September 6, 1957, while Haiti was still under the thumb of dictator-for-life François (Papa Doc) Duvalier. During her childhood, she lived in a middle-class part of Port-au-Prince and spent holidays in her mother's hometown of Jacmel. Her father, Roger Jean, principal and teacher at an upper-class Protestant preparatory school, insisted she be educated at home because, at school, she would have had to swear allegiance to Duvalier. Roger Jean was arrested and tortured.

In 1968, when Michaëlle was 11, the family fled to Canada as refugees. They settled in Thetford Mines, Quebec, the centre of one the largest asbestos mining regions in the world. Roger Jean found work teaching at a local college. But having survived the outrages of Haiti, he was, by this time, what his daughter called a "broken man." The marriage of Luce and Roger came apart, and Michaëlle moved with her mother and her sister to a basement apartment in Montreal. As Michaëlle described it, "all we could see looking out of our window was the feet of people passing by." Her mother supported the family by working in a clothing factory and as a night orderly in a psychiatric hospital. It's a testament to Luce's courage and determination that she saw to it that her children were well educated.

The future Governor General proved to be an exceptional student. After earning a Bachelor of Arts degree in Italian and Hispanic languages and literature at the University of Montreal, she pursued her master's studies in comparative literature and taught at the university's Faculty of Italian Studies. While in university, from 1979 to 1987, she worked at a women's shelter that was a model for the establishment of similar institutions for women and children across Canada. During that time, she managed a study on women as victims in abusive relationships, published in 1987.

Her Excellency Michaëlle Jean, Governor General of Canada, at a reception announcing the initiative of the Michaëlle Jean Chair in Canadian Caribbean and African Diasporic Studies, with Denham Jolly (left), the first Black owner of a Canadian radio station

She also contributed her efforts to organizations with a mandate to assist immigrants trying to enter Canada. Jean worked for a time with what was then Employment and Immigration Canada and at the Conseil des Communautés culturelles du Quebec.

She continued her education at the University of Florence in France and in Italy at the University of Perugia and the Catholic University of Milan. A talented linguist, Jean is fluent in Spanish, Italian and Haitian Creole as well as French and English. She reads Portuguese.

In 1988 she began a career in broadcasting and journalism at Radio Canada, the French iteration of the CBC.

She soon won acclaim as the host of a variety of news and public affairs programs, including *Le Point, Virages Actuel* and *Montréal ce soir*. Working effortlessly in both official languages, she hosted a number of programs on the English CBC, including *The Passionate Eye* and *Rough Cuts*. Her star rising, she hosted her own show, simply called *Michaëlle* in 2004, at the same time anchoring the French news channel RDI's *Grands Reportages*, and on occasion, anchoring the network's major newscast, *Le Téléjournal*. Like Adrienne Clarkson, her predecessor as Governor General, Jean was a respected broadcast journalist with a long and secure career ahead of her. She had married filmmaker Jean-Daniel Lafond, and the couple produced a number of films on social issues, including the award winner, *Haiti in All of Our Dreams*. The couple adopted a daughter, Marie-Éden, an orphaned child from Haiti.

Her life was settled and the future was bright.

Everything changed when Prime Minister Paul Martin called to ask if she would accept the post of Governor General. On August 4, 2005, the country was stunned by the official announcement that the Queen, on the recommendation of the prime minister, had appointed Jean to succeed Adrienne Clarkson as Governor General of Canada. Jean was the third woman, after Clarkson and Jeanne Sauvé (it's fascinating that all three women had had journalistic careers at the CBC), and the first refugee as well as the first person of Caribbean origin to hold the vice regal post. Jean is also the first representative of Queen Elizabeth II to have been born during her reign. Michaëlle Jean was invested as Canada's 27th Governor General on September 27, 2005.

The reaction across the country was, in most quarters, one of astonished delight.

But while most Canadians were pleased and inspired by Paul Martin's choice, others had misgivings. Gilles Duceppe, leader of the Quebec-based Bloc Quebecois, a party created to advocate for the separation of Quebec from Canada, said that he was disappointed that Jean had chosen to "accept a position that is strictly honorary and within an institution that is not democratic." Others questioned her involvement in her husband's films during the 1990s, which were perceived by some as having separatist leanings. On August 11, 2008, the *Globe and Mail* fanned the flames, reporting on a forthcoming piece for *Le Quebecois,* a sovereignist publication, that accused Jean and her husband of having supported independence for Quebec.

Some members of parliament as well as a number of provincial premiers demanded that the couple clarify where their sympathies lay. Prime Minister Martin felt called upon to issue a statement that the Governor General–designate and her spouse had both undergone thorough background checks by the Royal Canadian Mounted Police and the Canadian Security Intelligence Service, standard procedure for high-level appointments. Late August 2008 polls indicated that there had been a drop in public approval of the appointment. The Haitian community rose to her defence, among other things holding church services to support her.

With her marriage to Jean-Daniel Lafond, who was born in France, Jean had acquired dual French and Canadian citizenship, which further led some to question her loyalty to Canada. In response, the still new Governor General replied:

> I wish to tell you unequivocally that both my husband and I are proud to be Canadian and that we have the greatest respect for the institutions of our country. We are fully committed to Canada. I would not have accepted this position otherwise…[We] have never belonged to a political party or the separatist movement.

She renounced her French citizenship.

When she was invested at a special ceremony in the Senate chamber, Jean, in a moving speech, said, "the time of two solitudes that for too long described the character of this country is past." The motto on her personal coat of arms is *briser les solitudes*, meaning "breaking down solitudes."

It was never going to be easy. As she settled into her mandate, the Governor General won the hearts and the approval of increasing numbers of Canadians. But on November 11, 2005, when her car approached the National War Memorial in Ottawa for the Remembrance Day Ceremonies, a handful of veterans attending the event, still believing that she and her husband were separatist sympathizers, turned their backs in a gesture of contempt.

She soldiered on, travelling to communities across the country, presenting the Grey Cup, showing solidarity with the Inuit by eating seal meat, addressing the Alberta legislature, being honoured with an honorary degree by the University of Alberta, visiting (against the advice of government officials) Canadian troops in Afghanistan and creating a website that launched an online chat with Canadians. On a trip to five countries in Africa—Algeria, Mali, Ghana, South Africa and Morocco—in November 2006, she was taken to the point of disembarkation from which slaves were transported to America. A poignant photograph in her office shows her from the back, looking through a doorway of a building into which slaves were herded before being packed like sardines onto ships heading for the "New World."

Controversies continued, even well into her tenure. During a foreign trip in 2009, she was introduced as Canada's Head of State. Immediately, government officials, including Prime Minister Stephen Harper, took pains to remind her that the Queen of England was Head of State, and that Jean was merely her representative in Canada. Alex Himmelfarb, Clerk of the Privy Council at the time, reportedly described her as a "loose cannon."

No one mentioned that when the prime minister lost the confidence of the House of Commons in December 2008, he approached the Governor General on December 4, asking her to prorogue parliament so that he could avoid facing a formal vote of confidence the following Monday. There is no record that Michaëlle Jean, Head of State or not, consulted the Queen in the process of making her decision to save Harper by proroguing parliament until January 26. The Liberal opposition underwent a change of leadership during the period, the political stars took on a new alignment and Harper's government survived.

Michaëlle Jean is an incandescent agent of change, making unprecedented contributions to the creation of Canada. Like another agent of change, Barack Obama, she faces all of the obstacles erected by those who feel threatened by any deviation from the status quo that might change the balance of power, because power is what real change is always about. Perhaps her most important contribution is as a role model for young minority women and girls. It is my belief that a new generation, led by women, will make the greatest contribution to the creation of a new, more egalitarian Canada.

CHAPTER EIGHT

THE MODERN AFRICANS: REFUGEES, SCHOLARS AND ENTREPRENEURS

Most Canadians would be surprised to learn that close to 25 percent of the population of Brooks, Alberta, is made up of African refugees and immigrants. Even fewer know that some 5000 Nigerian Canadians live in Calgary. Over the past two or three decades, there has been a quiet influx of immigrants from modern Africa.

They have settled in widely separated parts of the country. Immigrants from French-speaking countries from Benin to Cameroon to Cote d'Ivoir to Mali to Senegal and Togo have settled in Quebec. If you want a taxi in Fort McMurray, the odds are your driver will be an African immigrant. Several African countries are represented in Toronto's diverse populations. Many Canadians have learned to tell the difference between Somalis and Kenyans.

When Lakeside Packers opened a meat-processing plant in Brooks, Alberta, they needed workers who could handle one of the toughest jobs a human can do. Killing and cutting up cattle and pigs is backbreaking, smelly and, for some, soul-searing work. Injuries are not uncommon, and the pay is low. In 2007 the company, which is southeastern Alberta's largest private sector employer, processed more than 1.3 million cattle. Needless to say, Lakeside was unable to recruit the labour it needed from the local population. Brooks started out as a village in 1910, growing through the years to town status. The population grew to more than 13,000 in the first decade of the 21st century. Until recently, it was a typical Alberta town, proud of its heritage based on the hard work of the original settlers who carved a living out of the land. And, like most small towns in Alberta, the population was almost exclusively white.

In 1969, Lakeside Packers became part of Canadian-owned XL Foods Inc., the largest beef processor in the country, with facilities in Alberta, Saskatchewan, Nebraska and Idaho. At the beginning, the company processed about 50 cattle per hour. But by the mid '80s the plant was handling 1000 cattle per day, about one-third of the total for all of Canada.

The plant employed refugees and immigrants from a variety of war-torn African countries. And in 2007, with complaints that they were not allowed to take bathroom breaks, were unable to file claims if they were injured on the job and were harassed by supervisors, the workers went on strike. The strike lasted for 24 days and led to the formation of a union. A CBC *Newsworld* program, "24 Days in Brooks," put the story in the national spotlight.

In the spring and summer of 2008, I chaired a task force on human rights, sponsored by the Calgary-based Sheldon Chumir Centre for Ethics in Leadership, which travelled to many centres in Alberta to hold hearings on local concerns. In Brooks, a year or so after the strike, with a new mayor, Martin Shields, in office, we found that the town had been remarkably transformed. There were certainly pockets of prejudice and discrimination, particularly in housing and some public services, but a team of local social agencies was working hard to address the issues. Our first meeting with representatives of various social, law enforcement and municipal organizations was so successful that the mayor invited us to return. "More people need to be part of this," he said.

Brooks has become, arguably, the most diverse community in Alberta, calling itself "The City of 100 Hellos." Workers at the packing plant, whose union was represented at our meetings, said the environment at the plant had improved, and most of their members were happier at work. A shop steward said that, because of the union, "people are not afraid anymore to bring up their concerns, they're not afraid to go to a doctor, that they'll be fired."

But what struck me as the most poignant development was the way that the community had adjusted to the new demographic. People understood the needed economic benefits that the plant and its workers represented. They understood that the workers were not going to "go back to where they came from"—that they were Canadians and fellow citizens. And, led by an enlightened young mayor, Brooks has changed from a white, socially conservative town to a place where hijabs (the traditional covering for the hair and neck worn by Muslim women) are commonplace, where grocery stores feature foods previously unheard of and where downtown bars feature African music. You might hear as many as 90 different languages on the street.

Brooks is a remarkable example of the creation of a new Canada that is learning to cope creatively with dramatic demographic shifts in its population.

THE NIGERIANS

When Canadians think about Nigeria, what often comes to mind are Internet scams, to which almost anyone with a computer has been exposed, and, more recently, attempted acts of terrorism. We have vague notions about a country that has had its share of turmoil—something about a war with Biafra, military coups and questionable elections.

Nigeria is the most populous and most diverse country in Africa. When I attended a conference on multiculturalism in the capital, Abuja, in the late 1990s, I learned that the country had more than 250 ethnic groups and more than 500 living languages or dialects. The common language is English because members of different tribes cannot understand each other's languages. A group of Canadians was invited to the conference because of our country's perceived success in managing diversity.

Few realize that Nigeria has one of the largest film industries in the world. There is Hollywood, Bollywood, and in Nigeria, Nollywood, which is ahead of the U.S. but behind India.

An outstanding example of one Nigerian who is contributing to the creation of Canada is Jude Igwemezie, PhD.

JUDE IGWEMEZIE

Jude Igwemezie comes from a family in which education has quasi-religious status. His late father, who had won a scholarship to study in Germany, was a professor of chemical engineering at Nnamdi Azikiwe University. His mother, a retired primary school teacher who runs an integrated school for handicapped children in their village, preached the value of education to her offspring. Jude, born on January 23, 1960, is the second of five children. An older brother, Linus, is executive vice president of oncology, with Novartis, an international pharmaceutical company. Another brother, Benjamin, is a nephrologist in High Point, North Carolina.

Jude Igwemezie won a scholarship to pursue his post-secondary education in Canada. He chose to come to Lakehead University in Thunder Bay, Ontario, because it was close to the largest freshwater lake in the world. He arrived in September 1978 and was shocked by the reality of the Canadian winter.

The next year he transferred to McGill University in Montreal and completed degrees in civil engineering and applied mechanics. In 1988 he joined Queens University as a research associate at the Canadian Institute of Guided Ground Transport and as an adjunct professor of civil engineering. His education led him to become an expert in railway track technology, and in 1989, he became the manager for track structure research at the institute. In 1991, having qualified for professional engineering (P.Eng.) status in Ontario, he went into private practice, soon becoming a widely recognized expert witness for inquiries into train derailments and track failures.

A dedicated entrepreneur, he operates three companies: Applied Rail Research Technologies (ARRT); NorFast, created to market products developed by ARRT, including elastic fasteners for railway tracks; and TransGlobim International Inc., a new company created in 2009 to take his expertise and products into world markets.

TransGlobim achieved major international success with an August 2009 contract to build a monorail people mover system in Iraq. The monorail will be built in the Muslim holy city of Najaf in Iraq and will link the three holy and historic mosques of Imam Ali, Kufa and Sahle. Transportation between the sites, visited as part of annual pilgrimages by many thousands, has been congested and inefficient. The project will create jobs in both Canada and Iraq.

Like his parents, Jude Igwemezie is a dedicated proponent of the importance of education. He tells the story of how his mother pushed him to take his studies to the highest level:

> I remember visiting Nigeria in 1982 following my undergraduate diploma and mom woke me up one morning at 5 AM. She sat on the edge of my bed and said to me: "Son, I have one request of you and will never ask you to do any other thing for me as long as I live." Eager to please mom, I quickly accepted. Well, she asked me to go back to school if they will accept me and study until I got a PhD. That was easy I thought.

His mother not only wanted to make sure that Jude would do well but she also used his promise to embarrass his older brother, who had only achieved a bachelor's degree. Her mocking drove him to take up new studies at the University of British Columbia. In addition to earning a PhD while working with Bristol Meyer Squibb, he obtained an MBA from Wharton School of Business in Pennsylvania.

A proud Canadian, Jude Igwemezie lives in the Greater Toronto Area with his wife, Donette, and twin children. It's likely that his greatest contributions to his adopted country are still ahead of him. His groundbreaking research into how to improve efficiencies in the operation of railroads are likely to come to the fore, as Canada, in the age of environmentalism, looks to the transportation system that united the country in the 1880s to reduce our carbon footprint in the 2010s.

ISA AND AMINA ODIDI

The husband and wife team of Isa and Amina Odidi both received their PhD in pharmacology and are acclaimed as leading scientists in their field. Isa received his BSc degree in pharmacy, his MSc in pharmaceutical technology and his PhD in pharmaceutics from the University of London. He is also a graduate of the Western Executive Management Program and obtained his MBA from the Rotman School of Management at the University of Toronto. Amina received her BSc in pharmacy, her MSc in biopharmaceutics and her PhD in pharmaceutics from the University of London. Isa and Amina both demonstrate a determined commitment to gender equality.

The Odidis immigrated to Canada in July 1995 and formed IntelliPharmaCeutics, a Toronto-based company that specializes in the design, development and marketing of controlled-release drug products. IntelliPharmaCeutics, which began full-scale operations in 1998, recently joined with a company called Vasogen Inc. to take the company public. It is now listed on both the Toronto and New York Stock Exchanges. The new company holds a number of patents for proprietary drug delivery technologies. Dr. Isa Odidi and Dr. Amina Odidi together own approximately 55.3 percent of the combined company.

Isa, who was born May 29, 1956, in Katsina, northern Nigeria, is chairman and CEO of the company while Amina is president and COO. They are a storied couple with royal roots. "My wife and I are of African royalty heritage, and I hold a title that is like that of a prince or a king," says Isa.

From 1995 to 1998, Isa Odidi was first the director then the vice president of Research of Drug Development and New Technologies at Biovail Corporation International

Entrepreneur Dr. Isa Odidi, who, with his wife, Dr. Amina Odidi, operates a successful pharmaceutical company listed on both the Toronto and New York Stock Exchanges

(now Biovail Corporation), a drug delivery company. Prior to 1995, he held senior positions in academia and in the pharmaceutical and health care industries. He currently holds a chair as professor of pharmaceutical technology at the Toronto Institute of Pharmaceutical Technology in Canada and is an adjunct professor at the Institute for Molecular Medicine in California.

Still connected to affairs in his country of birth, Isa Odidi was a candidate in the 2007 presidential campaign in Nigeria. It's Canada's gain that he did not win. Home in Canada, he champions democracy and human rights and has developed a reputation as a generous philanthropist.

Isa is a member of the influential Global Leadership Foundation, a group of world leaders with 20 former heads of government, including former Canadian Prime Minister Joe Clark. The foundation offers expertise in conflict resolution and nation building. Calling on the experience of its members, the organization offers private consultations to heads of state trying to resolve sticky national issues. Isa is also a member of the board of directors of the Canadian Council on Africa, which facilitates and promotes business transactions between Canadian and African companies. Isa and Amina Odidi were the recipients of a Harry Jerome Award for technology and innovation.

For Canada, Nigeria's most important export may be highly educated people such as the Igwemezies and the Odidis—people with strong entrepreneurial skills. The transition to Canada is easier for Nigerians than for many other Africans because Nigeria's official language is English.

A large number of Nigerians may have come to Alberta because oil production is a major part of both their economies. Perhaps it's because Calgary's surprising and recent diversity is welcoming to new players. On September 26, 2008, I attended the official opening of Nigeria House in northeast Calgary. A community centre for Calgary's growing Nigerian community, Nigeria House is a well-equipped, fully renovated property that was completely funded by a community of doctors, lawyers and engineers, as well as entrepreneurs who have joined the action in the Alberta oil patch. The facility includes a 2000-square-foot main hall, ultra-modern kitchens and bathrooms as well as several offices and boardrooms. Some 300 registered families form the core of the Nigeria House membership.

The official opening was a gala affair with the Nigerian ambassador to Canada headlining the ceremonies. Several members of the community hold academic posts at Calgary's educational institutions. The first Black bank manager in Calgary, Walé Gbalajobi, is also a member of Nigeria House.

But the Nigerian population in Calgary, like many other Black communities across Canada, faces challenges of isolation. Individuals and many ethnic groups tend to operate in their own silos, not knowing of the contributions that others whose heritage they share are making to their adopted country. As the Nigerian High Commissioner to Canada, Professor Iyorwuese Hagher said in a 2008 speech to the Nigerian Canadian Association in Toronto, which was celebrating the 48th anniversary of Nigerian independence:

> In my one year in Canada, I have come to realize that many Nigerians in Canada have refused to identify with any Nigerian group and have been submerged in their daily engagement and toil, to pay their bills and or train

their kids through school. Some of these individuals have a high net worth economically, but they have said goodbye to Nigeria, and any thought of associating with other Nigerians here in Canada is a source of unending pain.

Or, in more scholarly terms, as Korbla Puplampu and Wisdom Tettey put it in their book, *The African Diaspora in Canada*:

> Over the last few years, the world has witnessed an unparalleled intensification of, and expansion in, transnational migration. It has been estimated that by the mid-1990s, more than 100 million people had taken up residence in countries different from those in which they had been born....With transnational migration reaching unprecedented levels in Canada, the need for new trajectories of intercultural understanding and minority-relevant policy has never been greater.

Contemporary immigration has brought about a half million Africans to Canada. However, with some exceptions, they are scattered throughout the country, with, in many cases, few intercultural relations. This new and growing wave is likely to have a different and even more profound impact on the creation of 21st-century Canada than the immigration of slaves early in our history or the Caribbean "invasion" of the 1970s and '80s.

While earlier waves of immigration never really threatened the dominance of the old white male establishment, accelerating demographic and economic changes in the new century will almost certainly see a redistribution of power, particularly as Canadians with origins in China and India develop burgeoning clout in the business world. They will inevitably open the door to greater participation by other ethnic minorities, including Blacks.

The African Diaspora Association of Canada was formed in 2005 by the Association of Higher Education and Development (AHEAD) and the South African Rainbow Association to "foster value-adding contributions to Canadian society, and to form sustainable partnerships that directly benefit deserving African communities in Africa and Canada." The organization's goals include poverty reduction, human rights, gender equality, peace and social justice. The association, set up as an umbrella organization, had its official launch in Ottawa in June 2008, with significant attendance from the federal government. Many other groups are working under and outside of the umbrella to create positive experiences for immigrants. But the real challenge, according to Governor General Michaëlle Jean, is to build bridges between the often inward-looking silos that separate too many Canadians.

JOHN AKABUTU

A distinguished member of the African Diaspora in Canada is also a world leader in stem cell research, Dr. John Akabutu.

John Akabutu came to Canada from Ghana to study medicine at the University of Alberta. He is a professor of pediatrics and the head of pediatric hematology at the University of Alberta School of Medicine in Edmonton. His work in unravelling the mysteries and the uses of stem cells has led to some remarkable advances in medical science. Stem cells are "unprogrammed" cells that have the ability, when transplanted, to transform themselves into a variety of more specific cells within the body, with the potential to do everything from re-growing organs to mediating the development of certain types of cancer.

Dr. John Akabutu has done groundbreaking work in the recovery of stem cells from the umbilical cords of newborns.

Stem cells are used for bone marrow transplants, for gene therapy and for a variety of genetic and acquired diseases.

Dr. Akabutu's team has developed methods to purify, freeze and store stem cells from the umbilical cords of newborns. The use of stem cells from umbilical cord blood has been able to resolve a matter of considerable controversy among religious groups and medical ethicists who oppose taking stem cells from human embryos. The concern, most forcefully expressed by pro-life groups, is that taking stem cells requires the destruction of the embryo, which, they argue, is entitled to protection. Others believe that stem cells taken from surplus embryos as the result of in vitro fertilization, donated with consent, should not be a problem.

Dr. Akabutu's solution of harvesting stem cells from umbilical cords does not violate the sacredness of human life. Father Mark Miller and Rebecca Davis-Matthias, Edmonton-based Catholic ethicists, believe there is a substantial moral difference between getting stem cells from embryos and getting them from the umbilical cords of newborns.

Expectant mothers in Alberta are urged to donate the umbilical cords of their infants to the Alberta Cord Blood Bank, through which stem cells are used mainly in treating leukemia in children. It is Canada's only public cord blood bank.

"This is a labour of love," said Dr. Akabutu. "I can see the future for this thing and the future is immense."

Dr. Akabutu is also celebrated as the originator of a program that, since 1978, has provided high-quality comprehensive care, as well as education and support, for people suffering from hemophilia. In 2004, in recognition of his work, the Northern Alberta Comprehensive Hemophilia Clinic was renamed the Doctor John Akabutu Centre for Bleeding Disorders. He is recognized as one of the 100 Greatest Edmontonians of the 20th Century and has been recognized by the Alberta Medical Association with a medal for distinguished service.

Proud of his home country, John Akabutu serves Ghana as the honorary consul general for Alberta, Saskatchewan and Manitoba. He hosted a gala celebration of the 50th anniversary of Ghana's independence in 2007, with Her Excellency Dr. Ivy Amoakohene, the Ghana High Commissioner to Canada, as the guest of honour. Dr. Amoakohene presented him with a special award on behalf of the Ghana Friendship Association of Edmonton. Dr. John Akabutu's contributions to advancements in medical research have potential not just in Canada but also worldwide.

Chapter Nine

Icons and Trail-blazers: Movers and Shakers in the 21st Century

C anada has been created by extraordinary individuals who opened new doors and paved the
way to a better life for all kinds of people. In our
great diversity, every ethnic and cultural group celebrates icons whose courage and determination, often
against seemingly insurmountable odds, have made
our country a world example of a society whose citizens
have successfully found ways to live and work together
in reasonable harmony. We know that we are far from
perfect. Racial, gender and economic inequities still
stand on our toes. Too often. But it is part of the character of the great majority of us to strive for a more
open, more accommodating society. It begins with
tolerance—a term many don't like. Who indeed, wants
to be tolerated?

On this continuum (see next page), tolerance is
where most Canadians find themselves, most of the time,

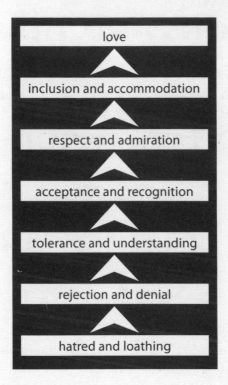

My relationship continuum

when they encounter minorities. It's useful, as a matter of perspective, to note that when Canadians talk about ethnic minorities, they are almost always thinking about people of colour. One never hears the term "ethnic Europeans." Nevertheless, many members of minority groups make their contribution simply by demonstrating that they can stay the course, do the job, carry the load—showing that there is nothing mysterious or exotic about them, nothing to be feared. Those who excel in their chosen vocations reveal to the world that they can be as good as, or better than, anyone else.

So here, in no particular order, is a survey of Black Canadians who have made or are making significant contributions to the creation of Canada. They are people that all Canadians should know about.

LINCOLN MACCAULEY ALEXANDER

No account of Black Canadian trailblazers is complete without the extraordinary story of the Lincoln Alexander.

In 1988, Alexander, then lieutenant-governor of Ontario, was invited to open the National Forum on Multiculturalism in Broadcasting. Organizers of the event expected a few fitting, carefully chosen words from the viceregal dignitary. Instead, Lincoln Alexander launched into a tirade against the national broadcasters who had been called to the forum, berating them for their "foot dragging" reluctance to properly reflect Canada's diversity in front of and behind the cameras and microphones. Alexander's statement was typical of the independent stand that had come to characterize the first Black to be appointed to the role of lieutenant-governor in Canada, a stand he put on record in his acceptance speech. He said:

> I hope I will be supported if from time to time I can't resist addressing the aspirations of our youth, and the concerns of the many, who, for whatever reasons, are not in the mainstream of life in Ontario. In these areas, I have strong convictions and intend to speak about them, as befits my office, in a dignified but forceful whisper.

Lincoln Alexander was born in Toronto to West Indian parents on January 21, 1922. His father, who came from St. Vincent, was a carpenter, but in those days, he took the only half decent job available to Black men: a railroad porter. Lincoln's mother, who came to Canada from Jamaica, worked as a maid under an early version of the West Indian Domestic Scheme. She had a powerful influence on Lincoln, always pushing him to get the best possible education. Her admonition of "Go to school, you're a little black boy," became the title of his autobiography, published in 2006, just short of his 85th birthday. In introducing the book, he said:

> Throughout my life I have believed thoroughly in the power of education, and that belief is the grand gift my mother, Mae Rose, gave me. The title of this book, the quote "Go to school, you're a little black boy," is hers, and I have used it to honour her insight and wisdom. Those words, her words, have been at the core of what I have accomplished in this life. She was a mere maid, but her knowledge and foresight transcended her station in life; she knew that accepting defeat was easy, but success was possible, and education was the vehicle to take you there. She was right, and it has. My education has always been my empowerment.

What Lincoln Alexander accomplished in his life is monumental. He grew up in modest circumstances in Toronto, spending a few years in New York before enlisting in the Royal Canadian Air Force in 1942. After being demobilized, he moved to Hamilton and completed a bachelor's degree in political economics at McMaster University. He also earned a degree in law at Osgoode Hall in 1953. But getting the opportunity to actually practice law did not follow easily. Like many Black lawyers before and after him, he had difficulty getting articled—the process that precedes being admitted to the bar and being recognized as a full professional. Established law firms did not open their doors to him. Finally, in 1954, he joined Miller, Tokiwa and Isaacs in Hamilton, the first interracial law firm in Canada. He became a partner in the firm in 1962 and was appointed Queen's Counsel in 1965.

The Hon. Lincoln Alexander (right), the first Black lieutenant-governor in Canada, with the author

Through it all, his deep concerns and involvement in community life led him to politics. In 1968 he ran against the tide of Trudeaumania and became the Progressive Conservative member of parliament for Hamilton West, holding the seat through four elections until he stepped down in 1980. In 1979 he was appointed minister of labour in Joe Clark's short-lived government, becoming both the first Black to be elected to the House of Commons and the first to serve in a federal cabinet. In parliament, Alexander supported the official languages act, fought for immigration reform and called for relief for Biafra in the Nigerian civil war. Older parliamentarians still remember that it was Lincoln Alexander who called Prime Minister Pierre Trudeau on his infamous "fuddle duddle" remark in the House of Commons, talking to the media outside of the immunity of the House about the "alleged" profanity.

After retiring from politics, Alexander took up a post as chairman of the Ontario Workers' Compensation Board, a position he held until 1985, when, on the recommendation of Prime Minister Brian Mulroney, he was sworn in as the lieutenant-governor of Ontario, serving until 1991. In 2000 he chaired the Canadian Race Relations Foundation, later becoming a member of many boards of directors, both in the corporate and non-profit worlds. He was the honorary patron of the Hamilton branch of St. John Ambulance and was established as honorary chief of the Hamilton Police Service.

The Honourable Lincoln Alexander holds the rank of Companion, the highest level within the Order of Canada. He is a recipient of the Order of Ontario and was the longest serving chancellor of the University of Guelph, holding the post for five terms, from 1991 to 2007, conferring degrees on more than 20,000 graduates. The university presented him with its inaugural Outstanding Leader Award, an annual honour that will always bear his name. The university also maintains the Lincoln Alexander Medal of Distinguished Service and the Lincoln Alexander Chancellor's Scholarships.

In 2006, Hamilton named him the "Greatest Hamiltonian of All Time." And the honours kept coming. In August 2009, at the age of 87, he was awarded the 2009 Couchiching Public Policy Award for his lifelong work toward the creation of a socially just and diverse society. He holds honorary doctorates from the University of Toronto (1986), McMaster University (1978), the University of Western Ontario (1988), York University (1990), Royal Military College (1991) and Queen's University (1992).

A bust of Lincoln Alexander is on display at the Hamilton Art Gallery. Few Canadians, of any ethnicity, have contributed so much to their country and been so heartwarmingly recognized.

LEONARD AUSTIN BRAITHWAITE

Leonard Braithwaite has the distinction of being the first Black to be elected to a provincial legislature in Canada. Born in Toronto of West Indian parents on October 23, 1923, he served as a Liberal member of the Legislative Assembly of Ontario from 1963 to 1975.

During World War II, Braithwaite saw action overseas with the Royal Canadian Air Force. After the war he earned a Bachelor of Commerce degree from the University of Toronto in 1950 and followed that up with a Harvard MBA in 1952. He returned to Canada to study law at Osgoode Law School, graduating in 1958. He was named Queen's Counsel in 1971.

While practicing law, he entered municipal politics in 1960, winning election to the Etobicoke Board of Education. Following a term in that office, he ran and was elected as an alderman to the Etobicoke Council in 1962. With that experience under his belt, and with a growing reputation as an effective representative of the people in his constituency, he decided it was time to run for provincial office. In a disputed election that saw him lose by 500 votes when the ballots were first counted, a re-count resulted in him winning the seat by 443 votes.

Twice re-elected, he was the labour and welfare critic for the Liberal Party and was instrumental in revoking Ontario's public school racial segregation laws. The practice of providing separate schools for Black children had been around in Ontario since 1850, when the Upper Canada Common Schools Act was passed. The final repeal of statutes legalizing racial segregation in both Ontario and Nova Scotia did not take place until the mid-1960s.

After being defeated in the 1975 election, Braithwaite returned to municipal politics, serving for a time on the Metro Toronto Council.

In 1999 Leonard Braithwaite was made a bencher of the prestigious Governing Council of The Law Society of Upper Canada. In 1997 he was inducted as a member of the Order of Canada and was appointed to the Order of Ontario in 2005.

JEAN AUGUSTINE

I didn't run as a black politician, I ran as a competent woman who is Canadian.

–Jean Augustine

Jean Augustine was the first Black woman to be elected to the House of Commons and the first to serve in the federal cabinet. No Black who succeeded in Canadian politics has had an easy time, but the road travelled by Augustine was more arduous than most. She was born on the island of Grenada, then still part of the British West Indies, in the community of Happy Hill, St. George's, on September 9, 1937. Her father, Ossie Simon, who worked on a sugar plantation, died before her first birthday. Her mother, Olive, was pregnant and had meagre resources, but the family was taken under the wing of a village matriarch known to all as "Granny." It was the kind of community where everyone looked after everyone else, especially children, and Granny, herself childless, was well off.

As Jean grew up, the emphasis on the importance of education was clear and unequivocal, and being bright and naturally curious, she excelled at school, winning a scholarship to a Roman Catholic school where she earned top grades. In high school she hosted a local radio program for teens and found time to organize an all-girls band.

Graduating a year early, Jean obtained her first job as a schoolteacher. On Sundays she wrote letters for members of her community who were not literate but wanted to keep in touch with relatives who had left the island to try their chances in other countries. The experience led to her decision to follow suit to try to find a better life overseas. In 1959, at the age of 22, Jean Simon came to Canada through the only means available at that time. She came on a West Indian Domestic Scheme visa to be the nanny for the children of a Toronto pediatrician. The program required her to stay in the job for a year, after which she could begin the process of becoming Canadian.

Fortunately, the family recognized her intellectual ability and supported her move into the outside world, helping her to find office work with a medical billing firm. Jean looked after the children by day and took night classes at the Toronto Teacher's College. After graduation, she was hired as an elementary schoolteacher in the city's school system, soon rising to the position of vice principal and then principal. She continued her education and earned a master's degree in education from the University of Toronto. In 1968 she married Winston Augustine. The couple had two daughters, Valerie and Cheryl, but divorced in 1981.

Jean, who throughout her life had demonstrated remarkable energy, threw herself into community service. She volunteered at the Hospital for Sick Children and on municipal task forces on drug abuse and crime. She hosted the first meeting of the Grenada Association in her apartment and was part of the group that put together the first celebration of Caribana during Canada's centennial year.

She became an active member of the Liberal Party and, in 1985, was part of the transition team as Premier David Peterson took office. Peterson appointed her the chair of the Metro Toronto Housing Authority, a position she held for six years.

During the run up to the 1993 federal election, Jean Chrétien, aware of her contributions and ability, bypassed the nomination process and made her the Liberal candidate in the riding of Etobicoke-Lakeshore. It's not hard to surmise that the appointment had a hint of tokenism. Of 65,000 voters in the riding, only 700 were Black. That made her victory all the more stunning. She garnered 19,458 votes, 42 percent of the total, beating her Conservative Party rival by 5152 votes.

Many Canadians will remember Jean Augustine sitting directly behind Prime Minister Chrétien during Question Period after he made her his parliamentary secretary, with, among other things, the responsibility to answer questions on his behalf when he was not in the House. She held the position from 1994 to 1996, when she was appointed Minister of State for Multiculturalism and the Status of Women. During her time in Parliament, she served three terms as chair of the National Liberal Women's Caucus and chair of the Standing Committee on Foreign Affairs and International Trade. She was the founding chair of the Canadian Association of

Parliamentarians on Population and Development, chair of the National Sugar Caucus, chair of the Micro-credit Summit Council of Canadian Parliamentarians, chair of the Canada-Slovenia Parliamentary Group and chair of the Canada-Africa Parliamentary Group.

Augustine gave up her seat in 2005, endorsing Michael Ignatieff to run in her place.

Since leaving electoral politics, she has maintained a high level of involvement in an incredibly diverse range of community service. She has served on the board of trustees for the Hospital for Sick Children; the boards of The Donwood Institute, which operates a centre for addiction and mental health; the Harbourfront Corporation; and has been national president of the Congress of Black Women of Canada.

Her hometown in Grenada presented her with a plaque that reads, "From Happy Hill to Parliament Hill," perhaps the honour she holds dearest to her heart. Her many other awards and honours include the YWCA Woman of Distinction Award, the Rubena Willis Special Recognition Award, the Kaye Livingstone Award, the Ontario Volunteer Award, the Pride Newspaper Achievement Award and the Toronto Lions' Club Onyx Award. In 2007 she was honoured by the University of the West Indies with a Caribbean Luminary Award.

Not ready for retirement, in 2007, Jean Augustine accepted a position as Ontario's first Fairness Commissioner, an arms-length agency with a mandate to ensure that immigrants with foreign professional qualifications are treated fairly. In Ontario, as in many regions of Canada, foreign professionals are too often found driving taxis or working at other jobs far below their abilities. The office administers the Fair Access to Regulated Professions Act, passed in 2006 to require professional associations to fairly review the qualifications of immigrants.

An important part of Jean Augustine's life is her relationship with York University, where she has served as a member of the board of governors. Her papers, including her Parliamentary Chair from the House of Commons, are lodged with the university.

York has created the Jean Augustine Chair in Education in the New Urban Environment in the Faculty of Education. The endowed chair will enrich a multitude of activities at York University with research and academic expertise in the areas of educational policy and practice, immigration, community engagement and cultural diversity.

Jean Augustine continues to make groundbreaking contributions to the creation of Canada by opening the doors for Black women to become full participants in the political life of the country.

ZANANA L. AKANDE

A city as large and culturally diverse as Toronto owes whatever success in racial harmony it enjoys to the constant vigilance of its citizens, its officials and its organizations.

–Zanana Akande

Zanana Akande holds the distinction of being the first Black woman to serve as a cabinet member in Canada. She was the first Black woman elected to the Ontario Legislature as a member of the government of Bob Rae.

When her parents, from St. Lucia and Barbados, came to Toronto in the mid-1930s, their qualifications as teachers were not recognized. Blacks were simply not allowed to hold teaching positions at that time. It was not until after World War II that a few Blacks, such as Denham Jolly, educated in Canada, were able to get teaching certificates. So Zanana's parents settled into Toronto's Kensington Market neighbourhood and found other ways to make a living, vowing that their children would have a better experience.

Zanana, born in 1937, grew up in what was then the city's most multicultural district (the mix included Jews and Chinese) and went to school at Harbord Collegiate before earning Bachelor of Arts and Master of Education degrees at the University of Toronto. After attending the Ontario Institute for Studies in Education, she did what her parents were not allowed to do and began her teaching career with the Toronto District School Board, eventually becoming a school principal.

But it wasn't easy. She had been a student teacher at the George Syme Community School and after graduation was hired as a full-time teacher. She was shocked when she was asked to eat her lunch in the basement, rather than in the school's staff room with the other teachers. Outraged, she reported the incident to the school authorities and was told that the situation would be resolved. It wasn't good enough. She refused to eat with her professional colleagues and took her lunches off the school's property.

As a principal she worked with inner-city schools with the first waves of the diverse populations that animate Toronto's schools today. She was particularly interested in children with special needs and worked to design programs to accommodate them.

Since her teens, Akande has been interested in social justice issues, and she found a political home in the Commonwealth Cooperative Federation (CCF), forerunner of today's New Democratic Party. She worked with the party's youth movement, sometimes acting as a scrutineer during elections.

Akande was encouraged to run in the 1960 provincial election but didn't expect to win, wanting simply to broaden the discussion. To her surprise, on September 6, she was elected to represent the riding of St. Andrew–St. Patrick and was appointed Minister of Community and Social Services in Bob Rae's new NDP government. She played an active role, serving on numerous committees and, in November 1992, was made parliamentary assistant to the premier. She oversaw the design and implementation of the Jobs Ontario Youth Program, creating more than 5000 summer jobs for students, from 1991 to 1994.

Akande successfully championed the introduction of employment equity legislation, but her particular interest while in government was the education of children with mental, physical or emotional challenges. She argued for their inclusion in the school system and other community institutions rather than have them segregated into institutions that could not facilitate their participation in society at large. Akande resigned from cabinet in 1994 after a dispute with the premier on a matter of principle. She did not run in the April 1995 election and returned to her role as a school principal, continuing her efforts on behalf of children with disabilities. She became increasingly involved in community affairs as president of the Urban Alliance on Race Relations as well as president of both the Canadian Alliance of Black Educators and the Toronto Child Abuse Centre. She volunteered with the United Way of Greater Toronto, the Elizabeth Fry Society and Doctors Hospital. And she also co-founded *Tiger Lily*, a local newspaper for visible minority women.

Zanana Akande continues her active involvement in community affairs. She has been president of the Harbourfront Centre and has served on the boards of the YWCA and of Centennial College. She is a founding member of the board of directors of Milestone Radio, which created Canada's first urban music radio station, Flow 93.5, in Toronto.

She is the recipient of many awards, and deservedly so, including the African Canadian Achievement Award for Education, the Congress of Black Women's Award of Distinction and the Constance E. Hamilton Award for her contribution to dealing with issues of equity. (Constance Hamilton [1862–1945] was the first woman member of Toronto City Council.)

HARRY JEROME

In the 1960s in the face of great adversity, Harry Jerome, the fastest man in the world, earned the respect of his country, not because of what he looked like or where he came from, but because of what he accomplished. The following excerpts from my book, *Running Uphill*, sum up his life as well as anything I could write now:

> Harry Winston Jerome, blessed with a perfect runner's body and driven by a compelling need to prove his worth, was born to be a winner. It's instructive to our understanding of him that, in runners' terms, his talent didn't blossom until relatively late in life. As he said, "As a juvenile, I couldn't beat anyone."
>
> Harry came from a troubled minority family. But their trials and triumphs were not so different from those of thousands of other Canadian households. It wasn't until he was 17, in the fifth year of his teens, old as sprinters go,

that he experienced the growth that transformed him from a gangly kid into a superbly smooth runner. By that time, the perplexing sense of being forever an outsider had surely rooted itself deep in his psyche. He was a Black kid stuck in a white world. His first, most devastating rejection came when he was still a vulnerable kid. But he was old enough to understand a situation from which his family could not possibly have sheltered him.

Neighbours drove him and his family out of the neighbourhood. He had to be painfully aware, as he matured, that his father had spent his life working in a job [as a railroad porter] that demeaned him, that his parents had wrenching disagreements about where and how to live and bring up their family, disagreements that ultimately led to family break-up. His self-defensive pride left him embarrassed when his only brother turned out to be marked by that terrible label, "retarded." His family was hardly a role model for marital success. His sister Carolyn left home at an early age. Louise [a younger sister] spent part of her young life in foster homes. His only Black friend, Paul Winn, was so surprising self-assured that he felt diminished in comparison.

And then, figuratively, he woke up one day and had to begin the process of coming to terms with the fact that he was fast, really fast—so fast that the whole world would know his name. He must have been stunned by his God-given talent. He had already learned that acceptance was never a sure thing, that he would have to prove himself again and again. No one—not his family, not his friends, not his coaches and manager, and certainly not the sports establishment—could ever feel the pressure to excel or the pain of failure as keenly as he did. His whole sense of self-worth was wrapped up in the need to win. All elite runners race against the obstacles in their lives.

Harry Jerome (second from right), the fastest man in the world through much of the 1960s, with one of the slickest comedians in the world, movie star Bob Hope

Harry hated to lose. His only option for success, in life and on the track, was to win, against all odds, and to win big. Everyone who knew him understood that losing at any-thing—chess, badminton, board games, cards—was an option he was incapable of contemplating. And while reality prevailed, allowing him to grudgingly concede when he had to at least pretend to concede defeat in ordinary games, his runner's body and his incredible need to validate himself gave him a hand equivalent to a royal flush whenever he stepped onto the track.

He learned to see his opponents as enemies. I don't think that Bill Bowerman, his Oregon coach, had to drill the idea of hating your competitors into his mind. Like his Olympic predecessor, Ray Lewis, who in every race ran against his bigoted high-school principal and his coach, Harry was quite candid in declaring his "hate" for anyone

211

he was running against. Losing only made him work harder, harder and harder, as hard as it took to prove to the world and, more importantly, to himself, that he really was a winner. There is no evidence that this "competitive hatred" went beyond the track. While, along with most of the people who lived in the high stratosphere of sports, he was not above doing things to "psyche out" his competitors, off the track, he liked and stood up for them. He was often a supporter and mentor of younger, emerging athletes. At the 1968 Olympics, Jerome was one of the those who protected swimmer Elaine Tanner, another teenage phenomenon, when she was hounded by reporters after failing to win a gold medal. And Harry's friends stood up for him, coming fiercely to his defence when the press savaged him.

"Really good athletes are really quite self-centred," John Minichiello (his long time coach) told me. "I don't mean self-centred in a negative way. He was good with his friends, but friendships wouldn't interfere with what he had to do. The focus was running and doing well. He was self-centred a little like the way Ray Charles, in the movie *Ray,* is self-centred. Great athletes are the same way."

And it's no stretch to understand why Harry was, throughout his life, extraordinarily modest about his accomplishments. He was never a braggart.

Harry Jerome retired from competitive running at the old sprinter's age of 28, with an Olympic bronze medal, gold medals from both the Commonwealth and the Pan Am Games around his neck and scores of prizes from track events around the world. He had been lauded for having made the greatest comeback in sports history. He knew how to get the things he needed, how to garner support for his causes, for which he was becoming an increasingly articulate spokesman.

Had he lived, Harry Jerome would have left an even greater legacy as an activist. As a young man, he went out of his way to avoid controversy, but in midlife, he knew how to pick his spots, how to use his fame to win his battles, to make things happen. He had already begun, at both the federal and provincial levels, to build a track record as a great motivator whose influence on kids could change their lives.

I've often wondered what kind of coverage the event might have had if he had lived to give the inaugural keynote address at the first Achievement Awards in March 1983, the Harry Jerome Awards. He would, first of all, have been respectful. But by then Harry had lost a good deal of the reticence that had kept him from speaking his mind. He had a much clearer idea of what he wanted to do with the rest of his life.

He would advocate on behalf of youth, particularly youth from ethnic minorities, and champion the need for inclusion, for facilities, for support for underprivileged kids in places like Toronto. He would call on the sports establishment to be more balanced in their coverage—and not build promising youngsters up, only to tear them down if they failed to meet expectations. He would challenge the hockey establishment of the day to open the doors to Black athletes challenging the myth that Blacks had skinny legs and did not have the ankle strength to be successful in hockey.

He would have expressed pride in the accomplishments of icons such as Lincoln Alexander and many others but would have noted that they were still the exception that proved the rule. Above all, his humility and his realism about his place in the world would have won him a whole new group of fans in the Black community from which he had been more or less estranged for most of his life. And that might have added a whole new dimension to his life.

Harry Jerome died of a seizure on December 7, 1982, at the age of 42. His unique contribution to the creation of Canada continues, as year after year he inspires the recipients of the Harry Jerome Awards, at the largest and most prestigious event celebrated by Canada's Black community.

Harry Jerome's story has been transformed to film. The National Film Board of Canada commissioned a brilliant young director to make a feature documentary of Jerome's life and times.

THE MAGNIFICENT HILLS

> We have not reached the promised land of the just society; so long as the rights of one person are abused, abridged or abrogated. Then the freedom of all is in peril.

> –Daniel G. Hill III

Few Canadian families are as star-studded as that of Daniel Hill and his two sons, Lawrence and Dan Jr.

Everyone knows the lyrics written by Dan Hill that contain the words "the honesty's too much" and what is arguably the best book about the Black experience (*The Book of Negroes*) written by Lawrence Hill, which will be soon be appearing as a feature film.

Daniel Grafton Hill III was born on November 23, 1923, in Independence, Missouri. His father, Daniel G. Hill II, was pastor of the African Methodist Episcopal Church, and he had a fierce dedication to education.

Daniel Grafton's mother, May Edwards, was a social worker. Like many families employed in the church, they endured a number of moves, and young Daniel grew up primarily in Colorado, Oregon and California. He completed his undergraduate education at Howard University and, following in his father's footsteps, he did a stint in the then highly segregated U.S. Army.

Hill moved to Toronto in 1950 and enrolled in the sociology program at the University of Toronto, completing his master's degree in 1951 and a PhD in 1960. His groundbreaking dissertation, "Negroes in Toronto: A Sociological Study of a Minority Group," has been widely cited by both scholars and advocates researching the history of Blacks in Canada.

Like many Blacks who carved their careers in mainstream society, Daniel Hill married into the mainstream. In 1953 he was teaching at a college in Baltimore when he met and fell in love with a white woman, Donna Mae Bender, who had been active in organizing civil rights sit-ins. The couple faced the same disparagement that Harry Jerome and his wife, Wendy, faced in Eugene, Oregon. Hill and his bride soon returned to Canada where the couple had three children, Dan Jr., Karen and Lawrence.

In 1955 Daniel was appointed head of the research department for the Metro Toronto Social Planning Council and served until 1959, a position later filled by Wilson Head, another Black Canadian icon. Hill was executive secretary of the North York Social Planning Council (1958–60) and assistant director of the Alcoholism and Drug Addiction Research Foundation (1960). He also lectured in the department of sociology at the University of Toronto (1961–62).

Daniel Hill made his most significant contributions to the creation of Canada when he was appointed the first director of the Ontario Human Rights Commission in 1962, becoming executive director of the newly created institution, the first in Canada, in the following year. He resigned the post in 1973 to enter private practice as a human rights consultant, advising a wide range of governments and organizations, ranging from the provinces of British Columbia and Nova Scotia and the government of Bermuda to the *Toronto Star,* the Canadian Labour Congress, the Canadian Human Rights Tribunal and the Metro Toronto Police Complaints Board.

Daniel G. Hill & Associates was essentially a family firm operating out of his home, with his wife, and son, Lawrence, comprising the "associates." It was the first human rights consulting firm in Canada. In addition, he served as advisor to the president of the University of Toronto on human rights and civil liberties and to the Ontario Attorney General on the subject of sects and cults. He was also a member of the Ontario Task Force on Legal Aid.

Recognized as a dynamic figure in the development of human rights, Daniel was appointed to the prestigious role as the province's first ombudsman in 1984, a position he held until retiring, at 65, in 1989.

In addition to his impressive record of employment, Daniel Hill had a powerful effect on the Black community in Ontario through a wide variety of extra-curricular activities. In 1978, with his wife and Wilson O. Brooks, he founded the now prestigious Ontario Black History Society, for which he served as president from its launch in 1978 to 1983.

Daniel's 1981 book, *Freedom Seekers: Blacks in Early Canada,* was the first book on Black history in Canada written for a general audience. It was approved for use as part of the high school curriculum in a number of provinces. With resources from the book, the Black History Society produced a travelling exhibit and later the first Black historical film, *A Proud Past, A Promising Future.* The half-hour educational film was widely used in schools. His training manual on race relations, written for the Metro Toronto Police Service, also saw wide circulation.

In 1993, Hill was part of the creation of the first Canadian celebration of Black History Month, now commemorated across the country.

Daniel Hill had been diagnosed with diabetes when he was 43 but kept the diagnosis to himself. The disease finally claimed him on June 26, 2003, a few months short of his 80th birthday. He had many awards, including an honorary doctor of laws from St. Thomas University and the Order of Ontario. He was made an Officer of the Order of Canada in 1993.

An intimate and revealing account of the life and times of Daniel Hill can be found in a poignant book by his son, otherwise known as one of the most successful musicians and composers in Canada, Dan Hill. The book, *I Am My Father's Son: A Memoir of Love and Forgiveness,* is tough and touching, both painful and humorous to any child of a strict, larger-than-life father who expected nothing less than perfection from his children.

When Dan was a teenager, practically hiding from his father in his bedroom, playing his guitar and writing songs, his father, who believed the only acceptable career for his offspring was that of a doctor, lawyer or engineer, said, "Time to face the cold hard fact, boy [he used "boy" in its most disparaging sense]. Accept your limitations. You're never gonna be a Bruce Cockburn."

Dan's brother, Lawrence, is the real writer in the family, but Dan felt compelled to write about his father, if only to come to terms with a difficult and often painful relationship.

Dan wrote, "If trying to win Dad over had been a big part of the driving force behind the forty-nine-year war between us, it had been a war I'd come to secretly enjoy as much as outwardly despise. The rivalry, the never-ending push and pull, the constant battles, helped define who I was. It was what drove me. And it was never supposed to end."

His own success has been phenomenal. Born in 1954, he grew up listening to the music of Frank Sinatra, Count Basie, Sarah Vaughan and Ella Fitzgerald. Dan started writing songs when he was 14, determined to carve out his own path in life. He was playing professionally in small venues by the time he was 17. He writes:

> At a very young age I realized I'd been blessed with two gifts. My first gift was musical: I had an unusually advanced ear for music and, more importantly, I had the soul for it. I'd also been gifted with a very, very good singing voice. My second gift was literary: I had a way with words. I wrote well. Ironically, I struggled with what schoolteachers coined at the time "reading comprehension." But when it came to writing stories, essays, articles—"how my family spent our summer vacation" type of stuff—my pieces were always singled out as the most well written, and the most interesting.

By the time Dan was 20, music had become his life, his "permanent day job." In 1972 he was signed by

RCA as a recording artist. His debut album was released in 1975 with songs such as "You Say You're Free" covered by scores of artists. "Sometimes When We Touch" is among the most covered songs in the history of modern pop music, with renditions by Tina Turner, Rod Stewart, Barry Manilow, Tammy Wynette, Lynne Anderson, Donny Osmond, Rodney Crowell, Roseanne Cash and Cleo Laine, who made it the title track of her 1979 album.

After a 20-year career as a singer-songwriter, Dan changed his focus, writing for successful stars such as Celine Dion, George Benson. Britney Spears and the Backstreet Boys.

His first attempt at writing a novel, called *Comeback,* was published in 1983. It failed, both critically and commercially—the worst critic, in hindsight, being Dan himself. But he learned from it. And his current book, *I Am My Father's Son,* is both gripping and literate. He says that a song he wrote on the theme of *I Am My Father's Son* is one of the best he has ever composed.

He has, at this writing, a Grammy, five Junos, four number-one songs, 12 top 10 records, four platinum albums and two gold albums, and his career is far from over. His songs are recorded by everyone from Celine Dion to Alan Jackson to Rod Stewart. And the music is still coming.

But in the writing department, it is Dan's younger brother, Lawrence, who is the star. Well educated in the family tradition, Lawrence has a bachelor's degree in economics from Quebec City's Laval University and a master's degree in writing from Johns Hopkins University in Baltimore. He worked as a journalist for the *Globe and Mail* and the *Winnipeg Free Press* while he was cutting his teeth as a novelist and nonfiction writer.

Lawrence's own story of his multiracial parents' lives, *Black Berry, Sweet Juice: On Being Black and White in Canada*, is a much more celebratory look at the challenges they faced than *I Am My Father's Son*.

Lawrence followed with novels, first, *Some Great Thing*, published in 1992, and, in 1999, *Any Known Blood*. But it was his third novel, *The Book of Negroes*, that was long-listed for the valued Giller Prize, won the Commonwealth Writers' prize for Best Book, the Rogers Writers' Trust Fiction Prize, the Ontario Library Association's Evergreen Award as well as CBC Radio's "Canada Reads." The book was also a finalist for the Hurston/Wright LEGACY Award and was long-listed for the IMPAC Award. *The Book of Negroes* is the gripping story of a girl captured for the slave trade and sent to America, eventually coming to Nova Scotia with the United Empire Loyalists and spending time as a celebrity in England before returning, full circle, to Africa. It is the most penetratingly articulate telling of the inner life of a woman who triumphed against all odds to retain her personal integrity.

The rights to *The Book of Negroes* have been picked up by Conquering Lion Pictures, and a movie to be directed by Clement Virgo is in the works.

Lawrence Hill has published a number of nonfiction books and writes for a variety of magazines, including *The Walrus*, currently the most successful literary magazine in Canada. His 2005 essay, "Is Africa's Pain Black America's Burden?" won the National Magazine Award. A television public affairs program that he wrote, called *Seeking Salvation: A History of the Black Church in Canada*, won the American Wilbur Award for best national television documentary.

In mid-career, Lawrence Hill is already a major figure on Canada's literary landscape. At this writing, he is hard at work on a new novel.

CHARLES OFFICER

Charles Officer is a bright rising star in the Canadian film industry. He is one of those rare gifted people who have an abundance of career choices and take a while to decide what they really want to do. Born on October 28, 1975, in Toronto's Grace Hospital, he is the youngest of four children born to Lonie and Herbert Officer. His father was born in England and grew up in west London before coming to Canada. His mother came from Jamaica by way of New York to study business in 1960 but worked as a nurse while her husband earned a living as an electrician.

Charles grew up in a multiracial community in East York in which the cultural mix included Greek and Italian descendents. As a teenager, he thought about being an architect. He began his post-secondary education at the Ontario College of Art and Design (OCAD), choosing sculpture as his major discipline. But he was also athletically gifted and left school to play professional hockey in England when, at the age of 18, he was drafted by the Calgary Flames and sent to their farm team in Salt Lake City, Utah. Uncertain about his prospects of actually playing in the NHL, Charles was sidelined by an injury, and he returned to school at OCAD. Along the way he discovered an interest in acting and found himself in a class with Clement Virgo and Sarah Polley, whose brilliant career involves several major acting roles as well as producing and directing the award-winning movie, *Away From Her*.

Now writing as well as acting, Officer was invited to study at the Canadian Film Centre, the increasingly prestigious institution founded and supported by expatriate Canadian film director Norman Jewison, whose Hollywood credits range from *Fiddler on the Roof* to *Jesus Christ Superstar* to *A Soldier's Story.* After writing and directing a number of well-recognized short films, Officer created *Nurse, Fighter Boy*, a poignant urban love story about the soul of a mother, the heart of a fighter and the faith of a child. The film has won rave reviews at festivals around the world.

But acting is still in Officer's blood, and he won acclaim in Canada's theatrical community when he played the Sidney Poitier role in *Raisin in the Sun*, the powerful play by Lorraine Hansberry that made its debut on Broadway in 1959. The Canadian revival, a 2009 co-production between Toronto's Soul Pepper Theatre and Theatre Calgary, was described by the *Hamilton Spectator* as "A glorious, soul-destroying production of Lorraine Hansberry's 1959 drama."

Charles Officer's latest film is a feature documentary about Harry Jerome, based on my biography of him, *Running Uphill.*

CLEMENT VIRGO

Another young Black Canadian filmmaker to watch is Clement Virgo. Born in Montego Bay, Jamaica, on June 1, 1966, he moved to Canada with his family in 1977. After finishing high school, where he developed an interest in fashion, he got a job as a window dresser. But his real dream had always been to direct films.

Clement applied to the Summer Lab program at the Canadian Film Centre in Toronto and was accepted into the inaugural program in 1991, returning the next year for a coveted nine-month residency. His first short film, created at the film centre, *Save My Lost Nigga Soul*, won the best short film categories at the Toronto and Chicago international film festivals as well as a Genie nomination. The film had festival "legs," winning the Paul Robeson Award for the best short of the African Diaspora at the 1995 Pan African Film and Video Festival. The film kick-started a career that is, at this writing, in full bloom.

His first feature film, *Rude,* which he wrote and directed, was a critical success. It was invited to the Cannes Film Festival, nominated for eight Genie Awards and played at the 1995 Toronto International Film Festival. A prolific writer-director, Virgo's filmography includes *The Planet of Junior Brown, Love Come Down, Lie with Me* and *Poor Boy's Game,* starring the American actor Danny Glover and Rossif Sutherland, son of Canadian actor Donald Sutherland.

But what many expect to be his greatest film will be *The Book of Negroes,* based on Lawrence Hill's award-winning and bestselling novel of the same name. Clement and producer Damon D'Oliveria have acquired the rights to the book.

Clement Virgo also has a growing list of television credits, including the 2009 NBC/CTV serial, *The Listener.*

MEASHA BRUEGGERGOSMAN

Not since Portia White has a Black Canadian opera star had such a worldwide impact. Interestingly, Measha Brueggergosman shares some ancestral roots with White. Measha's paternal great grandparents came to Nova Scotia with the United Empire Loyalists.

John and Rose Gosman, whose names are recorded in the original "Book of Negroes," were on the last ship to leave New York City for Halifax in 1783. The family settled in Fredericton, New Brunswick, where Measha was born on June 28, 1977, to Anne Eatmon and Sterling Gosman.

The family had a natural and traditional attachment to the church, and Measha's spectacular vocal gifts were evident from the beginning. She sang in the church choir as a child and took voice and piano lessons from the time she was seven. With encouragement and support from family and friends, she was able to take up more serious studies at the Boston Conservatory, continuing her studies at the University of Toronto where she earned a Bachelor of Music degree. Recognized for her superior talent, Measha spent five years in Germany, getting a master's degree at the Robert Schumann Hochschule in Düsseldorf.

Measha married her high school sweetheart, Markus Brüegger, a Swiss national who had come to New Brunswick as an exchange student, and the couple combined their names; hence Brueggergosman.

Measha soon rose as a bright star in the firmament of operatic music. At the age of 20, she played the lead role in *Beatrice Chancy*, an opera written by the librettist and poet George Elliott Clarke and composer James Rolfe. The opera, based in the era when Measha's grandparents had come to Canada, was presented nationally on the CBC. She has appeared throughout Canada, with the Toronto and Montreal symphony orchestras, the National Arts Centre Orchestra and the Thunder Bay Symphony Orchestra. She also has performed with the Cincinnati Opera and at the International Beethoven Festival in Berlin, at Carnegie Hall in New York and before Queen Elizabeth at the Royal Albert Hall in London, England.

In 2005 Measha was a featured soloist in a recording of William Bolcom's *Songs of Innocence and Experiences*, which won three Grammy Awards, including Best Classical Album. She won the Grand Prize at the 2002 Jeunesse Musicales Montreal International Music Competition, as well as prizes at the Wigmore Hall International Song Competition in London, England; the George London Foundation in New York; the Queen Sonja International Music Competition in Oslo, Norway; and the ARD International Music Competition in Munich, Germany. In Canada she won the 2008 Juno Award for Classical Album of the Year for *Surprise*. She is featured in the 2003 CBC documentary, *Spirit in Her Voice*.

Measha Brueggergosman was forced to take time off during the early part of 2009 because of a heart condition. But she returned to the stage in September 2009 for a bravura performance at the Toronto International Film Festival.

Her star still shines.

WILSON A. HEAD

Wilson Head's journey up to Canada from the deep south of America was nowhere near as arduous as those who travelled north on the Underground Railway generations earlier. He came comfortably to a respectable job in Windsor, Ontario. But the challenges he discovered in his new home made him keenly aware that life for Blacks in his new country was still far from easy.

Wilson Adnonija Head was born on a farm near Atlanta, Georgia, on September 13, 1914. His father, like many who came out of slavery in earlier generations and found it difficult or impossible to own their own land, was a sharecropper. Sharecroppers frequently found that, according to the landlord, the fruits of their efforts sometimes didn't even cover the cost of running the farm. Wilson's parents, Evander and Evelyn Head, were keenly aware that the only way out of their trapped existence was education. They made sure their son was well educated. He received a BSc in education from the Tuskegee Institute in Alabama, a Master of Social Work degree from the University of Chicago and, in 1958, a PhD in education and social science from Ohio State University.

Degrees in hand, Wilson stepped easily into leadership roles in Chicago as director of a community house program and as head of the Ohio State Juvenile Diagnostic Centre. He answered an ad in a social work magazine for an executive director of a group therapy project in Windsor, Ontario. The interview was a win-win, and Wilson and his wife, Phyllis, arrived in Canada in October 1959.

He was soon lecturing social work students at the University of Windsor, and as well, crossing the border to be a guest lecturer at the University of Michigan and at Wayne State University. In 1965 he moved to Toronto to become director of research and planning of the Social Planning Council of Metro Toronto and, almost immediately, became involved with a variety of advocacy groups.

Unlike discrimination in the U.S., which was direct and recognizable on its face, Canada's, and particularly Toronto's, discrimination was more subtle, but the result was equally daunting. It didn't matter whether a landlord told you flat out that he didn't rent to Blacks or said that he had just rented out the apartment—the outcome was the same.

With strong leadership capabilities, Wilson Head soon found himself involved with organizations such as the National Welfare Council and the Canadian Civil Liberties Association, of which, in 1967, he was the Toronto vice-president. He also was one of the founders of the National Black Coalition.

He became the first chairman of the Bachelor of Social Work Program at Atkinson College, a part of York University. A prolific writer, he authored a wide variety of articles and research studies, among them "The Black Presence in the Canadian Mosaic" and "The Adaptation of Immigrants."

Head was a co-founder and first president of the Urban Alliance on Race Relations, an active intervener and advocacy group based in Toronto with participation from a broad cross-section of mainstream and minority organizations.

He was awarded a Doctor of Laws degree from York University in 1982 and was an early recipient of the Harry Jerome Award. Wilson remained active in community affairs until his passing on October 6, 1993. In his book, *A Life on the Edge: Experiences in "Black and White" in North America*, a lengthy and fiery memoir, he wrote:

> For the first time in history many Canadian police departments are making a major effort to recruit women and people of colour or "visible minorities." School boards in the Toronto area are struggling with the vast influx of newcomers, many of whom are from developing or "third world" countries. Pressure has been brought upon local school officials to employ more Blacks and other

non-white teachers and administrators to serve as role models for the increasing numbers of non-white students in the various school systems...many Torontonians can claim that population changes have been relatively harmonious.

The statement serves as a fitting epitaph for a man who worked so hard to change the dynamics of how Canadian institutions such as police forces and boards of education treat minority members of the communities they serve.

HAMLIN GRANGE AND CYNTHIA REYES

Our city is blessed. For the most part it works. But a lot of people still feel left out and disengaged from the political process.

–Hamlin Grange

Hamlin Grange was one of the founders of the Black Business and Professional Association in Toronto. It was at his suggestion that the organization named its prestigious achievement awards after track star Harry Jerome. Born in Toronto of West Indian parents, Hamlin was one of the first Black broadcasters in Canada. His athletic talent won him a scholarship to study in the U.S., where he completed a degree in journalism at the University of Colorado. He broke into journalism as a reporter for the *Denver Rocky Mountain News* but soon returned to Canada to become managing editor of *Contrast,* for years the voice of the Black community in Toronto.

He worked as a reporter for the *Toronto Star* before moving into television, with stints at the CBC, at

Hamlin Grange, one of the founders of the Black Business and Professional Association and one of the early Black broadcasters to work at the CBC

which he hosted national programs on *Newsworld*, the Global Television Network and TVOntario. He is one of the founders of the Canadian Association of Black Journalists. Among his awards is the B'nai Brith Human Rights Award for Journalism. He has served as a member of the Toronto Police Services Board, the Greater Toronto YMCA's Board of Directors and the Ontario Provincial Police Commissioner's Community Advisory Committee.

Hamlin is married to Cynthia Reyes, who has crafted an equally prestigious career in media. Starting out as a newspaper reporter, she moved into television, winning many honours as a producer and director at the CBC. In 1990 she took on the role of training CBC journalists, winning the corporation's President's Award and the Crystal Award for Outstanding Achievement in Film and Television. Born in the Caribbean, Cynthia claims that she comes from the "world's most multicultural family." She has been recognized by Canadian Women in Communications as Trailblazer of the Year and has received the African Canadian Achievement Award and the Children's Broadcast Institute Award.

In 2000 Grange and Reyes formed DiversiPro, a consulting company that specializes in diversity training for employers and employees. One of the company's major annual initiatives is the Innoversity Creative Summit, which brings together international participants to explore ideas and solutions to the challenges faced by organizations operating in an increasingly multicultural society. Organizations need to reflect the communities in which they operate, in their staffing, in their advertising and in their sales policies. The couple leads workshops for senior managers in a wide range of enterprises in the private sector, as well as for people in law enforcement, media, health care and public service. Both acknowledge there is still a lot of work to do in this area.

JULIUS ISAAC

The creation of Canada has been enhanced by a small group of "cream of the crop" West Indian islanders, many of whose stories are told in this volume. They came to this country seeking higher education, bringing intelligence and discipline. While many maintained their connections to the country of their birth, most opted for Canadian citizenship—our gain, their home country's loss.

Julius Alexander Isaac, born in Grenada in 1928, whose passport was superior academic potential, arrived in Toronto in 1955. He worked his way through school, first taking a job as a maintenance worker at the *Toronto Star*, then going "on the road" as a sleeping car porter. While at university, he was a founder of the Grenada Association of Toronto and served as a director and treasurer of Toronto's Caribana Festival. Even before completing his law degree he acted as a legal advisor to the Canadian Brotherhood of Railway, Transport and Other Workers.

After graduation he was admitted to the Ontario Bar in 1960 but moved to Saskatchewan in 1962, where Tommy Douglas was creating medicare and making the province, from a social development point of view, one of the most exciting places in North America. Julius became legal advisor to the Economic Development Corporation of Saskatchewan.

Later in the 1960s, he returned to Grenada for a year-long stint as a senior magistrate. But in 1971 he was back in Canada working with the federal Department of Justice, achieving the coveted designation of Queen's Counsel in 1975. He served as a Crown prosecutor and rose to become the Assistant Deputy Attorney General of Canada.

Isaac was appointed as the leading attorney for the Ontario Securities Commission, and as his career blossomed, became a judge of the Supreme Court of Ontario in 1989. On December 23, 1991, Prime Minister Brian Mulroney confirmed his appointment as Chief Justice of the Federal Court of Canada, making him the first Black chief justice of any court in Canada. He served on the court for the next eight years, resigning, past his 70th birthday, on September 1, 1999.

But not quite retired, he travelled to Jamaica in 2001 to head a three-person inquiry into political corruption and gang violence. He also accepted an appointment as a member of the Court Martial Appeal Court of Canada.

Mr. Justice Isaac received many awards, including honorary doctorates, from the University of Windsor and the University of the West Indies, the Canadian Black Achievement Award in Law, the Silver Jubilee Award of Grenada and the Jackie Robinson's Distinguished Achievement Award. Governor General Michaëlle Jean presented him with the Order of Canada in 2006.

STANLEY G. GRIZZLE

> My name's not George.
>
> —Stanley Grizzle

In his 1998 autobiography, *My Name's Not George,* Stanley Grizzle chronicles the demeaning life of the Black men who worked for Canadian railways as sleeping car porters. At that time, wealthy tourists would call the porters, who tended to their needs 24 hours a day, "George." It was marginally better than being called "boy," but Grizzle bristled at the term. His rise from a porter to a citizenship court judge is a story of unrelenting belief in his own worth.

Stanley Grizzle was born in Toronto in 1918, the oldest of seven children of Jamaican parents who had come separately to Canada in 1911. His mother came as a domestic, his father as a railway worker. His father had a gift for entrepreneurship and saved enough money from his job to buy a taxi, eventually building a small fleet of cars and employing Black drivers. The family, moderately well off, always owned their own home, and the couple's children grew up in a relatively comfortable environment. Young Stanley went to King Edward School and to Harbord Collegiate. But when the Great Depression devastated the economy, the Grizzles were forced onto public welfare.

In June 1940, at the age of 22, Stanley went to work as a sleeping car porter and quickly became active in the Brotherhood of Sleeping Car Porters.

"Why did I get a job as a porter on the railway?" he asks in his book. "I couldn't get anything else—and I didn't want to starve....None of the department stores had any non-white people working for them and the City wouldn't even hire Blacks to clean the streets."

He served in the Canadian armed forces in Europe during World War II but returned to work on the railway, becoming president of his union local. He was, throughout his life, deeply involved in issues of racial discrimination, both on the job and in his community. He was part of a campaign that eventually convinced the CPR to allow Blacks to hold management positions, and he worked with the Joint Labour Committee to Combat Racial Intolerance. Stanley campaigned for the creation of the Ontario Fair Accommodation Practices Act and for the legislation that led to the creation of the Human Rights Commission, the first in Canada.

In 1960, after a failed run for a seat in the Ontario legislature, he worked for the Ontario Labour Relations Board. In 1978, Prime Minister Pierre Trudeau appointed him as a citizenship judge, a role that involves reviewing applications for Canadian citizenship as well as officiating at ceremonies at which new citizens take the Oath of Allegiance.

Judge Stanley Grizzle is a member of the Order of Canada and of the Order of Ontario.

HERBERT (HERB) H. CARNEGIE

> Herb Carnegie was likely one of the best ever players to never play pro-league hockey.

> —citation in Canada's Sports Hall of Fame

Had Herb Carnegie been born a couple of generations later than the early 1900s, there's little doubt that he would have been a member of the Hockey Hall of Fame, along with Jean Béliveau, with whom he played in the Quebec Senior Hockey League (QSHL). Carnegie's hockey career began with the Toronto Young Rangers in 1938, at a time when the idea of a Black man playing in the NHL was pure fantasy. Conn Smythe, who owned the Toronto Maple Leafs, frequently said that he would pay $10,000 to anyone who could turn Carnegie white. At that time, there was no one around like Branch Rickey, who broke baseball's colour barrier by signing Jackie Robinson in 1945. It wasn't until 1958 that Willie O'Ree joined the Boston Bruins and broke the NHL's colour barrier.

The son of Jamaican immigrants George and Adina Carnegie, Herb was born on November 8, 1919. He and his brother Ossie grew up in the Willowdale district of Toronto. They were crazy about hockey, listening to Foster Hewitt's legendary broadcasts of NHL games and spending countless hours on a local pond perfecting their hockey skills.

Herb, remembered as a smooth-skating centre, was restricted to playing in the minor leagues—in Perron and Shawinigan Falls in northern Quebec and in Sherbrooke. Playing alongside Ossie and another Black player, Manny McIntyre, Herb formed one of the most successful lines in hockey history. The three players were known as the Black Aces. Reed Storey, the Hall of Fame NHL referee, said:

> They were good enough as a line to play in the American League, which was a level below the NHL....It was strictly colour, not talent, that kept him out. The trio, of course, faced racial taunts, both from spectators and from opposing players. Herb, at centre, was the playmaker; Ossie, on right wing, had a bullet slap shot; and Manny had the muscle. He answered racist remarks with his fists, gaining them a certain amount of respect.

Herb was the league's MVP in 1946, '47 and '48. In 1948 he won the QSHL scoring title. While playing with the Quebec Aces in 1951, he and Jean Béliveau were selected to play on the league's all-star team. Both Béliveau and Frank Mahovlich, two of the NHL's great centres, were said to have considered Carnegie as one of the finest players of his time.

In his 1997 autobiography, *A Fly in a Pail of Milk*, Carnegie recounts the one time the door to the NHL was opened by a tiny crack. A letter from the New York Rangers arrived at his house unexpectedly, inviting him to the team's training camp at Lake Saranac, New York. The letter, he learned, had been sent to 20 amateur and semipro players. As he tells it, after out-performing the other players, he was called into the office and offered $2700 to play with the Rangers' lowest level farm team in Tacoma, Washington. Herb had made $5100 playing in Sherbrooke during the previous season. He turned down the offer. Various members of the Rangers' organization bumped the offer to $3700 and then to $4700. Carnegie still declined.

Some have called Carnegie's refusal to sign a mistake. Jackie Robinson had accepted a low-ball deal to play for the Montreal Royals and went on to make history. But for Herb Carnegie, it was a matter of pride.

After retiring from hockey, Carnegie became a successful businessman as a senior account executive with Investors Group. It was at this time that he found the game of golf, winning the Canadian Senior Gold Championships in 1977 and '78. He also became an advocate for young athletes, creating the Future Aces Hockey School for 12- to 14-year-old kids and building the Future Aces Foundation, which provides annual bursaries to enable youngsters to continue with post-secondary education.

Herbert H. Carnegie was appointed to the Order of Ontario in 1996 and made a member of the Order of Canada in 2003. He received a Harry Jerome Award in 2002 and was recognized with an honorary doctor of laws degree from York University in 2006. The North York Centennial Arena was renamed the Herbert H. Carnegie Centennial Centre in 2005. He was featured in two special issues of the *Spiderman* comic book, helping Spidey break up a hockey puck/drug smuggling gang, as well as foiling The Chameleon's plan to steal a valuable chemical formula.

The greatest hockey player the NHL never had is a role model well recognized for the programs he developed to support young athletes.

Oscar Emmanuel Peterson

He was the most famous Canadian in the world.

—Jean Chrétien, former prime minister of Canada

It was a cold, rainy night in Montreal in 1949. Norman Granz, the American jazz impresario who had almost single-handedly raised the public perception of jazz music to unprecedented levels, was in a taxi heading for Dorval Airport. The driver had the radio tuned to a live broadcast from the Alberta Lounge, a popular downtown Montreal nightclub. The music that emanated from the speaker was stunning, like nothing he had ever heard before. Absolutely captivated, he told the driver to turn around and take him to the club, arriving before the set had ended.

It was one of those serendipitous happenings that change lives and history. The music was coming from a piano played by Oscar Peterson, already known in Montreal as the best "boogie woogie" player around. Granz was the creator of the legendary "Jazz at the Philharmonic," a series of concerts at New York's Carnegie Hall that featured the likes of Ella Fitzgerald, Count Basie and Louis Armstrong. Recordings of the concerts are considered collector's items.

Granz invited Peterson to perform at Carnegie Hall, but, because of union regulations, Oscar could not be featured on the bill. The American Federation of Musicians, headed by the legendary (at least in music circles) James C. Petrillo, made and enforced strict regulations about non-union and foreign musicians playing in union halls. Peterson didn't have a work visa. So, part way through the concert, Granz called Peterson to come to the stage from his seat in the audience. The crowd was left gasping by the speed and dexterity of his playing. No one had played the piano with such facility since the inimitable Art Tatum, one of Peterson's greatest idols. According to a report in *Down Beat* magazine, Peterson "stopped the concert dead cold in its tracks." He was 24, and he had reached the pinnacle of the jazz world.

The rest, of course, is history. And what a history it is!

Peterson was born on August 15, 1925, and grew up in a house not far from the Union United Church, which anchored Montreal's Black community. His father, Daniel Peterson, like many who lived in what was sometimes known as "Little Burgundy," worked as a sleeping car porter. But he was also a musician who played trumpet and piano, and the Peterson house was filled with music. Daniel scraped together money to buy a piano and let his children know that he saw music as one way out of a life working on the railroad.

Oscar was five when he started to play the trumpet and the piano. The trumpet may have been his first choice, but respiratory problems forced him to put the instrument down. Oscar's older sister, Daisy, already an accomplished musician who became the teacher to many of Montreal's finest jazz musicians, including Joe Sealy and Oliver Jones, gave him his first piano lessons. And the lessons were classical. Oscar learned to read the language of music and to count. Further lessons with a Hungarian-born pianist, Paul de Marky, gave him the proficiency to bring his own sense of music to the instrument.

Oscar became totally caught up in the music, practicing four to six hours every day. By the time he was nine, he played with a level of control that astonished musicians. Jazz and ragtime began to creep into his repertoire, and at one stage he was known as "the Brown Bomber of Boogie-Woogie." He was only 14 in 1940 when he won a national CBC music competition, which impelled him to drop out of school and develop a professional career in music. He won first prize on the Ken Soble amateur show on the radio station CHCH in Hamilton. That led to a weekly radio show on the CBC network and guest appearances on shows such as *The Happy Gang*.

But he almost gave it all up when his father played a recording of Art Tatum's "Tiger Rag." Tatum's mastery of the instrument was so overwhelming that, at first, Oscar thought there was more than one person playing. "Tatum scared me to death," he said. "I was just about flattened…I swear, I didn't play piano for two months afterwards, I was so intimidated." He said he would "never be cocky again" about his own mastery of the instrument. Years later, the two met and became friends, but Peterson was always reluctant to be compared to his hero and avoided playing in Tatum's presence.

Norman Granz did more than put Peterson in the spotlight at Carnegie Hall; he became his friend and lifelong manager, helping the development of a 65-year performing career that made Peterson an authentic international star. He was the best in the world at what he did, a member of jazz royalty, or, as Duke Ellington put it, "The Maharaja of the keyboard." He made more than 200 recordings, won eight Grammy Awards and played literally thousands of live concerts worldwide.

Oscar played with the greatest musicians of his era; among them are Ray Brown, Coleman Hawkins, Ben Webster, Milt Jackson, Herb Ellis, Barney Kessel, Ed Thigpen, Niels-Henning Ørsted Pedersen, Stéphane Grapelli, Ella Fitzgerald, Louis Armstrong, Clark Terry, Joe Pass, Anita O'Day, Fred Astaire, Stan Getz, Canadian Dave Young and orchestra leaders Dizzy Gillespie and Count Basie. A complete list would fill several pages.

A prolific composer, Oscar Peterson has left a durable legacy. His "Hymn to Freedom" was performed by the San Francisco Boys Chorus and the San Francisco Girls

Chorus at the inauguration of U.S. President Barack Obama. His "Canadiana Suite" is frequently showcased. His "African Suite" was completed in 1979. In 1981 he composed "A Royal Wedding Suite," in honour of Prince Charles and Lady Diana. He wrote "City Lights" for the Ballets Jazz de Montreal, and his score for the Canadian movie *The Silent Partner* won him a Genie in 1978. His score for *In the Key of Oscar* won a Gemini Award.

When Peterson celebrated his 80th birthday, Diana Krall, in addition to "Happy Birthday," sang a vocal version of one of his songs, "When Summer Comes," with words written by her husband, Elvis Costello.

In addition to his eight Grammys, Peterson's awards include:

- The Juno Awards Hall of Fame
- The Canadian Jazz and Blues Hall of Fame
- The Roy Thompson Award
- The Toronto Arts Award for Lifetime Achievement
- The Governor General's Performing Arts Award
- The Glenn Gould Prize
- The Praemium Imperieale World Art Awards
- The UNESCO Music Prize
- The BBC-Radio Lifetime Achievement Awards

He was a Companion of the Order of Canada, the highest level of the award, restricted to 72 members at any given time. He was also a member of the Order of Ontario, the National Order of Quebec and an officer of the Ordre des Arts et des Lettres of France. The Oscar Peterson Concert Hall at Concordia University in Montreal was built in 1990 in his honour.

From 1991 to 1994, Peterson was the chancellor of Toronto's York University, which now hosts the Oscar Peterson Chair for Jazz Performance, endowed by the Government of Ontario. He was very proud when the Peel District School Board opened the new Oscar Peterson School, just over three kilometres from his home in Mississauga. He has been celebrated with 13 honorary degrees from universities in Canada and the United States.

His autobiography, *A Jazz Odyssey: The Life of Oscar Peterson*, was written in collaboration with jazz journalist Richard Palmer. Several documentaries have chronicled his life, including *In the Key of Oscar*, produced by his niece, Olympic athlete and film producer Silvia Sweeney.

Canada Post produced a commemorative stamp in his honour.

Oscar Peterson passed on quietly at his home in Mississauga on December 23, 2007. He was 82.

CHAPTER TEN

BLACK STUDIES

As we become more accepting of our diversity, and as more people from a wide variety of origins assume positions of influence and make meaningful contributions to the creation of Canada, we become increasingly comfortable with the many heritages that make up this country. But the fact that ethnic groups, who tended to be inward looking, share stories of their experiences in their new country is a relatively recent phenomenon. Although Canada was never a melting pot, where everyone is expected to assimilate into the dominant culture, the perception of our society as a "mosaic" could give the impression that everyone should keep their culture within the bounds of their particular "tile," which, in some cases, meant their ghetto. In a mosaic, each tile is different and separate. It is only when viewed from a distance that the whole picture becomes coherent.

When eastern Europeans came to the prairies in the 1920s and '30s, many tried hard to put their ethnic pasts behind them. They dropped the "skis," "itzes" and "chucks" from their names and insisted that their children speak English, even if they were themselves uncomfortable in the language. It took generations for their grandchildren and great grandchildren to revive an interest in their roots. In western Canada, courses in Ukrainian and many other languages have become regular elements in the school systems.

There was no option for visible minorities to blend into the British-defined mainstream. No amount of name changing could obliterate the second-class status of Chinese, Japanese and South Asian immigrants. Blacks who came from America or the West Indies, of course, had British names, given to them by the colonial masters who had brought them across the Atlantic from Africa. An Anglo name offered Blacks no passport into the mainstream.

But as we enter the second decade of the 21st century, the study of the achievement of minority groups is gaining academic legitimacy. A fascinating indicator is the emergence of research chairs at Canadian universities dedicated to the study of the origins and experiences of a wide variety of ethnic groups. For example, there are endowed chairs in Hungarian, Italian, Ukrainian, Estonian, Jewish, Islamic and Black studies. Queen's University has a Chair in Ethnicity and Multicultural Citizenship. There is a Canada Research Chair in the Comparative Study of Indigenous Rights and Identity. Ethnic studies have become a well-established academic discipline.

Academic chairs are usually endowed by funds coming from the private, government and academic sectors. Distinguished academics are appointed to the positions for a fixed term, during which they are expected to play a leadership role in fostering research and organizing seminars, symposia and conferences on relevant issues, and, in some cases, writing and teaching.

The first chair in Black studies was established at Dalhousie University in 1996, with a mandate to act as a catalyst for the creation of a Centre of Excellence in Black Canadian research, a clearinghouse for material relating to Black Canadian scholarship, as well as a centre for coordinating major local, national and international conferences on Black Canadian research. The chair sponsors research, awards scholarships and hosts conferences. A national conference, entitled "Multiple Lenses: Voices from the Diaspora located in Canada," was held in Halifax in October 2005. Noted writers, scholars, lawyers and community leaders, as well as politicians and other leaders made presentations to the 428 registered delegates.

Unfortunately, the work of the chair was impaired by a tragic accident that severely injured the incumbent, Professor David Divine. In March 2007, he was struck by a car while walking on a sidewalk and was hospitalized for several months. In addition to the loss of leadership, limited funding forced the university to curtail a number of the chair's activities. At this writing, Dr. Divine has sufficiently recovered from his injuries to resume his duties.

The Harriet Tubman Institute at York University is another example of an organization that is dedicated to capturing, studying and telling the story of the migration of African peoples around the globe, from centuries ago to the present day. The institute was launched on March 25, 2007, the 200th anniversary of the day the British law to abolish slavery received royal assent. The institute sponsors a wide variety of conferences, seminars and workshops. Harriet Tubman, who spent some time in Canada, was an iconic leader of the American Black struggle against slavery before and during the American Civil War. She arranged for more than 70 former slaves to travel to Canada through the Underground Railway.

The DaCosta-Angelique Institute, founded by Dolores Sandoval, PhD, is a Black think-tank based in Montreal that contributes to academic conferences on Black issues, particularly in Quebec.

In 2005, the University of British Columbia established the Centre for Culture, Identity and Education, a research centre that focuses on exploring issues of identity and their educational implications in local and international cultural contexts.

A new chair that will make a significant contribution to Black studies was created in 2009 at York University. The Jean Augustine Chair in Education in the New Urban Environment, part of the Faculty of Education, is designed to support Canada's next generation of teachers, educational leaders and researchers working to improve schooling in metropolitan cities.

The chair came into being at a time when issues surrounding the education of Black children in metropolitan Toronto were provoking a great deal of controversy. After years of battling to integrate minority students into the public school system, a struggle that reached back to the days of segregated schools, a new movement called for separate, Black-focused schools. Supporters were concerned about high dropout rates among Black students who, often with the support of their parents, felt that the curriculum was neither relevant to them nor met their needs. There was passion on both sides of the debate. One intervener pleaded, "Don't propose it—Martin Luther King thought we could sit at the front of the bus together....if Black kids need to graduate, let's get teachers in there and learn how to interact with Black kids." A community leader argued that she was alarmed by the high number of Black youth being "pushed out" of school by a European-centred system.

After a long and often bitter campaign, on January 29, 2008, the Toronto School Board voted 11–9 to open an alternative Africentric school to fight a 40 percent dropout rate among Toronto's Black teens. At a cost of some $820,000, the school was scheduled to open in September 2009. It would be open, school board trustees noted, to all students, regardless of colour.

In defence of the motion, trustee Shelia Ward said, "I don't know what it's like to be a Black parent, but I do know pain when I see it and recognize despair when I hear it, from the deepest part of the soul of those who believe time is running out."

The issues faced by minority groups, especially youth, in urban settings is one of the challenges the Jean Augustine Chair is designed to address.

The most recent academic chair concerned with the history, experience and potential of Black Canadians is the Michaëlle Jean Chair in Canadian Caribbean and African Diasporic Studies at the University of Alberta.

It is probably appropriate at this point for me to disclose my relationship with the Governor General. When Dr. Malinda Smith of the Faculty of Arts and Dr. Jennifer Kelly of the Faculty of Education put forward an initiative to create a chair in Black studies at the University of Alberta, they asked me to become involved. I suggested that the chair be named in honour of Michaëlle

Jean and subsequently asked the Governor General if she agreed. At a reception in Calgary, Jean put her hand over her heart and said that she would be honoured.

The Michaëlle Jean Chair in Canadian Caribbean and African Diasporic Studies will reside in the faculties of arts and education at the University of Alberta and will work closely with similar institutions such as the James Robinson Johnston Chair in Black Studies at Dalhousie University, the Jean Augustine Chair in Education for the New Urban Environment at York University and the Harriet Tubman Institute. The mandate is to bring academic rigor to the study of Canada's diverse Black community and to "accomplish original research into the Caribbean and African Diaspora's historical and contemporary experiences in Canada."

At a Toronto reception announcing the initiative on March 2, 2009, Her Excellency said:

> I believe that our greatest challenge in this day and age, already marked by the mingling of cultures, will be to transform yesterday's prejudices into tomorrow's opportunities....And I believe that the best way to achieve this is to take a clear look at the lessons of the past and reflect together on the issues of the present and the future.

I agreed to be a co-chair of a national fundraising campaign to endow the chair. Having read this far, you will not be surprised that my reaction to the appointment of Michaëlle Jean was one of unalloyed delight.

With the Governor General lending her name and enthusiasm, a campaign is under way to raise funds to endow the chair at the University of Alberta.

AFTERWORD

The Internet, in addition to being a rich information resource, can also change the way we read and learn. If you want to know more about a person, place or thing referred to in something you're reading, Google, Bing or Yahoo will take you there, though you need to be cautioned to double check everything. This is certainly true of the stories and incidents chronicled in this book. Far more information is available on most subjects than could be included here. But readers have the luxury of filling in any blanks by using the technology that is so profoundly changing the way we communicate, the way we think and the way we learn. There is no need to rely on your memory for facts—they are always there in cyberspace.

In writing *How the Blacks Created Canada,* I had to carefully monitor my own involvement in the story. I know or have met many of the people I have written about.

Some of them are friends and colleagues. Born in 1932, I have lived through a fairly large slice of the history of Blacks in Canada. In some small ways, I have been part of that rich history. I was fortunate to be the host/narrator of a seminal television series on the history of Blacks in Canada, Almeta Speak's *Hymn to Freedom*. In addition, over the years, I have developed a small but comprehensive personal library on Black issues.

So, as I'm sure you can plainly see, I did not come to the writing of this book as a dispassionate outsider. But I hope that my journalistic instincts have made me as objective as possible. One of the most daunting challenges was choosing which individuals, among the thousands who have contributed to the creation of Canada, should be included. I have no doubt made errors of judgement. For this I take full responsibility.

For the mainstream Canadians who are the primary target audience for this book, I hope you will gain a new appreciation of, and a new curiosity about, the role Black Canadians have played and continue to play in our astonishing country. For members of the scattered and diverse Black communities across Canada, I hope that, as you learn more about our remarkable history, you will focus as much on the accomplishments of your fellow Canadians as on the many mountains that remain to be climbed.

NOTES ON SOURCES

Abucar, Mohamed. *Struggle for Development: The Black Communities of North and East Preston and Cherry Brook, Nova Scotia, 1784–1987.* Halifax: Black Cultural Centre of Nova Scotia, 1988.

Adams, John. *Old Square Toes and His Lady: The Life of James and Amelia Douglas,* 1st ed. Vancouver: Horsdal & Shubart, 2001.

Akrigg, G.P.V and Helen B. Akrigg. *British Columbia Chronicle: 1847–1871.* Vancouver: Discovery Press, 1977.

Alexander, Lincoln. *Go to School, You're a Little Black Boy.* Hamilton: Dundurn Press, 2006.

Arnett, Chris. *The Terror of the Coast: Land Alienation and Colonial War on Vancouver Island and the Gulf Islands, 1849–1863.* Vancouver: Talon Books, 1999.

Bertley, Leo W. *Canada and its People of African Descent.* Pierrefonds, QC: Bilongo Publishers, 1977.

Best, Carrie. *That Lonesome Road: The Autobiography of Carrie M. Best.* New Glasgow, NS: The Clarion Publishing Company, 1977.

Brown, Hallie Q. *Homespun: Heroines and Other Women of Distinction.* Don Mills, ON: Oxford University Press, 1992.

Brown, Rosemary. *Being Brown: A Very Public Life.* Toronto: Ballantine Books, 1989.

Cahill, Barry. "The Colored Barrister: The Short Life and Tragic Death of James Robinson Johnston 1876–1915." *The Dalhousie Law Journal,* Vol. 15. No. 2, Fall, 1992.

Clarke, Austin. *Growing Up Stupid Under the Union Jack.* Toronto: McClelland and Stewart, 1980.

"Farewell to a political kung fu fighter." *Toronto Star,* June 15, 2003.

Fraser, Fil. *Running Uphill: The Fast, Short Life of Canadian Champion Harry Jerome.* Edmonton: Dragon Hill Publishing, 2006.

Grant, John. *The Maroons in Nova Scotia.* Halifax: Lorimer Books. 2003.

Grizzle, Stanley G. with John Cooper. *My Name's Not George: The Story of the Brotherhood of Sleeping Car Porters.* Toronto: Umbrella Press, 1998.

Head, Wilson. *A Life on the Edge—Experiences in "Black and White" in North America.* Toronto: University of Toronto Press, 1995.

Hill, Dan. *I Am My Father's Son.* Scarborough, ON: Harper Collins, 2009.

Hill, Lawrence. *The Book of Negroes.* Scarborough, ON: Harper Collins, 2007.

Hymn to Freedom (video). International Telefilm (5090 Explorer Drive, Mississauga, ON L4W 4T9; Ph: 905-629-3133) Toronto, 1994.

Katz, William Loren. *The Black West.* New York: Touchstone Books, Simon and Shuster, 1987.

Killian, Crawford. *Go Do Some Great Thing: The Black Pioneers of British Columbia.* Vancouver: Douglas and McIntyre, 1978.

MacEwan, Grant. *John Ware's Cow Country.* Vancouver: Greystone Books, Douglas and McIntyre, 1973.

Mifflin Wistar Gibbs. *Shadow and Light: An Autobiography—Mifflin Wistar Gibbs.* Reprinted from the original 1902 edition inscribed by the author. Lincoln, NE: Bison Books, University of Nebraska Press, 1995.

"Oppose Negro Immigration." *Edmonton Bulletin,* April 13, 1910, p. 8.

Ormsby, Margaret A. *British Columbia: A History.* Toronto: Macmillan Company of Canada, 1958.

Pachai, Bridglal. *Blacks: Peoples of the Maritimes.* Halifax: Four East Publications, 1987.

Pachai, Bridglal. *William Hall: Winner of the Victoria Cross.* Halifax: Four East Publications, 1995.

Palmer, Howard and Tamara Palmer. *Peoples of Alberta.* Saskatoon: Prairie Books, 1985.

Ruck, Calvin W. *Canada's Black Battalion: No. 2 Construction 1916–1920.* Halifax: Black Cultural Society of Nova Scotia, 1986.

Scott, Victoria and Ernest Jones. *Silvia Stark: A Pioneer.* Greensboro, NC: Open Hand Publishing, 1991.

Shepard, R. Bruce. *Deemed Unsuitable.* Toronto: Umbrella Press, 1997.

Taylor, Sheldon. *Bromley: Tireless Champion of Just Causes. Memoirs of Bromley L. Armstrong.* Pickering, ON: Vitabu Publications, 2000.

Tettey, Wisdom J. and Korbla P. Puplampu (eds). *The African Diaspora in Canada.* Calgary: University of Calgary Press, 2005.

Thompson, Colin A. *Blacks in Deep Snow: Black Pioneers in Canada.* Don Mills, ON: J.M. Dent & Sons, 1979.

Thompson, Colin A. *Born with a Call: A Biography of Dr. William Pearly Oliver, C.M.,* Halifax: Black Cultural Centre of Nova Scotia, 1986.

"Ward Chipman Papers." Library and Archives Canada. (microfilm copy available at NSARM, mfm. No. 10163, pp. 28–53).

Ware, John. *The Canadians*. Markham, ON: Fitzhenry and Whiteside, 2005.

Williams, Dawn P. *Who's Who in Black Canada*. Toronto: D.P. Williams and Associates, 2006.

Williams, Dorothy W. *Blacks in Montreal 1628–1986: An Urban Demography*. Cowansville, QC: Les Éditions Yvon Blais, Inc., 1989.

Winks, Robin W. *The Blacks in Canada: A History*, 2nd ed., Montreal: McGill University Press, 1997.

Web Sources

Annapolis Heritage Society. www.annapolisheritagesociety.com/hinotablerose.htm.

The Bukowski Agency. www.thebukowskiagency.com/More.htm.

Chinese Canadian National Council. www.ccnc.ca/cccop/index.php?section=content/history.php&func=viewEntry&entryID=59.

Dictionary of Canadian Biography Online. www.biographi.ca.

Documenting the American South. docsouth.unc.edu/neh/henson58/henson58.html#henso4 (*The Life of Josiah Henson, Formerly a Slave, Now an Inhabitant of Canada, Truth Stranger Than Fiction,* and later issued as *Father Henson's Story of His Own Life*).

The Kudzu Monthly. www.kudzumonthly.com/kudzu/dec01/Josiah_Henson.html.

FIL FRASER

FIL FRASER is a Canadian cultural institution with a career spanning more than half a century. Fraser made his mark in filmmaking, radio and television, as a writer and as a human rights activist.

His literary achievements to date include the bestselling memoir *Alberta's Camelot: Culture and the Arts in the Lougheed Years* and the biography *Running Uphill: The Fast, Short Life of Canadian Champion Harry Jerome*, now a National Film Board feature-length documentary.

Fraser currently serves as adjunct professor of Communications Studies at Athabasca University, Canada's pioneering distance-learning institution, where he teaches a graduate course on film policy. He is a former director of Telefilm Canada and was the former CEO of Vision TV. He also is a former chief commissioner of the Alberta Human Rights Commission.

For his long years of public service and accomplishment, Fraser was awarded the Order of Canada in 1991 and received an Honorary Doctorate from the University of Alberta in 2008.

Other titles from Dragon Hill Publishing

DRAGON
HILL

RUNNING UPHILL

The Fast, Short Life of Canadian Champion Harry Jerome
by Fil Fraser

This is the heroic story of a young black man who overcame crushing adversity to achieve national acclaim as an athlete and as a champion of human rights.

$18.95 • ISBN: 978-1-896124-13-1 • 5.5" x 8.5" • 240 pages

HOW THE FRENCH CREATED CANADA

From New France to French Canada
by Julie Perrone

From the early French explorers of the New World to modern debates over the status of Québec in the Confederation, the French role in the evolution of Canada has been deep and profound. This book explores the history, culture and contributions of the French Canadian community to Canadian society.

$18.95 • ISBN: 978-1-896124-18-6 • 5.25" x 8.25" • 248 pages

HOW THE ENGLISH CREATED CANADA

An Intriguing History of Explorers, Rogues, Fur Traders, Pioneers, Prime Ministers, Heroes and Soundrels
by Jeff Pearce

In the multicultural mosaic that is Canada, the English have had a defining role with their contribution of flamboyant personalities and hard-working settlers. Author Jeff Pearce examines the history of the English in Canada from their first discovery to modern-day constitutional tensions, using humour, insight and good-natured storytelling.

$18.95 • ISBN: 978-1-896124-20-9 • 5.25" x 8.25" • 240 pages

Available from your local bookseller or by contacting the distributor,
Lone Pine Publishing
1-800-661-9017
www.lonepinepublishing.com